Awaken. Align. Achieve. Ascend:

Trust. Transform. Thrive. Transcend

Embrace. Expand. Elevate. Empower

Focus. Forgive. Flow. Flourish

Alavida

Copyright © 2024 *Alavida*
Alavida Publishing

All rights reserved. No portion of this book may be reproduced, stored in a retrieval system, or transmitted in any form or buy any means - electronic, mechanical, photocopy, recording, scanning, or other, with the prior written permission of the author or publisher.
For inquires or requests, please contact the author at:
al@alavidapublishing.com

ISBN: 978-1-959602-47-7

This Book is Dedicated to the People
all over the World

Contents

Introduction: Awakening to Your True Potential 1
Discovering purpose and unlocking your true self.

1. **Understanding Your Inner Drive** 9
   Exploring purpose, passion, and meaningful goals.
2. **Cultivating a Growth Mindset** 23
   Shifting perspectives to embrace challenges as opportunities for growth.
3. **Mastering Self-Discipline** 37
   Building lasting habits through small actions and identity alignment.
4. **Emotional Intelligence and Success** 47
   Understanding emotions to improve relationships and decision-making.
5. **Living with Purpose and Inspiration** 59
   Aligning actions with your core values to fuel inner growth.
6. **The Art of Transformation** 71
   Harnessing optimism to reframe setbacks and stay motivated.
7. **Building Resilience** 81
   Learning how to thrive through adversity and failure.
8. **The Art of Decision Making** 91
   Making confident choices by balancing logic and intuition.
9. **Nurturing Creativity and Innovation** 107
   Fostering creative thinking to spark new ideas and solutions.

10. **Leadership and Influence** **121**
    Becoming a leader by inspiring and empowering others.
11. **Achieving Work-Life Balance** **133**
    Prioritizing what matters to create a life of harmony.
12. **Financial Wellbeing and Success** **145**
    Building financial habits aligned with personal values.
13. **The Journey of Continuous Learning** **157**
    Cultivating a mindset of lifelong learning and growth.
14. **The Digital Age and Personal Growth** **171**
    Using technology mindfully to enhance personal development.
15. **Envisioning and Realizing Your Future** **181**
    Turning dreams into reality through intentional actions.

Conclusion: Embracing the Journey of Transformation ... 195
Reflecting on the journey and continuing personal growth.

Further Reading: **202**

Introduction
Awakening to Your True Potential

Let your cup of life be full and overflow,
Let your soul take flight and your compassion grow.
In life you either boldly come out and play,
Or you hide in your comfort zone and there you stay!
The magic of life is found outside your comfort zone,
It's the fear you face, the fear you embrace, the fear you own!
— *Alavida*

Have you ever woken up and asked yourself, "Is this really the life I was meant to live? Is this really my life?" Maybe you've felt a quiet discontent, even after achieving everything you thought would make you happy. That's because most people live their lives in a kind of trance—a conditioned, automatic way of being shaped by early experiences, social expectations, and the environment we grow up in. From the moment we are born, we absorb beliefs, expectations, and limitations, many of which we never chose for ourselves. These unconscious patterns guide our actions, shape our thoughts, and influence every choice we make.
But what if the version of yourself that you've been living isn't who you truly are? What if the struggles you face—whether in relationships, career, or self-worth—aren't signs of inadequacy, but rather symptoms of living someone else's script?

This book isn't just another attempt to fix what's broken. It's an invitation to wake up from the hypnosis of everyday life, to step out of the patterns that have kept you stuck, and to embrace the full expression of your potential.

The Trance of Conditioning: Why Most People Stay Stuck

As children, we are deeply influenced by our environments. Small moments—disapproval from a parent, rejection from a peer, or a harsh word—can leave emotional imprints that shape how we see ourselves and the world. These experiences create a blueprint for our self-worth, setting the foundation for limiting beliefs that often go unquestioned well into adulthood.

Without ever realizing it, we fall into routines and identities handed to us, striving to meet expectations we never consciously chose. Many people spend their entire lives pursuing success, approval, or happiness, only to discover that no amount of achievement brings lasting fulfillment.

This happens because most self-help advice focuses on surface problems: how to think positively, set goals, or manage time. But true transformation begins when you go deeper—when you awaken to the unconscious patterns driving your behaviors and confront the root wounds that keep you stuck.

At the core of this process is understanding that many struggles —whether fear of rejection, perfectionism, or insecurity—stem from early wounds that have not been healed. The key to breaking free isn't more self-improvement but reconnecting with the real you—the part of yourself that exists beneath the layers of conditioning and pain.

Alex and Rachel: The Comfort Zone Trap

Alex and Rachel appeared to have everything. Alex had a high-paying job, a stylish home, and a growing network of friends. Yet each achievement left him feeling more restless than before. *"Is this all there is?"* he often wondered, but he kept chasing the next milestone, hoping it would bring the peace that always seemed just beyond reach.

Rachel had built her life around being perfect—perfect daughter, perfect employee, perfect partner. But no matter how hard she worked, she always felt like she was falling short. Her life was full, but she felt disconnected from herself and the people she loved.

For both Alex and Rachel, comfort had become a trap. The pursuit of security and external success kept them safe—but it also kept them stuck. They hadn't yet realized that the lives they were living weren't truly their own.

The Dissatisfaction Loop: Why We're Never Fully Happy

Even with external success, many people feel an underlying sense of dissatisfaction—a low hum of unease that follows them through life. Eckhart Tolle describes this as a background discomfort, which people try to escape through achievements, distractions, or consumption.

It's a cycle of "just one more thing"—one more promotion, relationship, or milestone—believing that happiness lies in the next accomplishment. But every time we reach that next thing, the dissatisfaction returns. This endless pursuit leaves us chasing but never arriving.

True fulfillment isn't found by acquiring more. It comes from learning to be present with what is—from embracing the wholeness that already exists within you. This book offers a new approach: not a race toward the next thing, but a journey inward to reconnect with the version of yourself that's already complete.

The Trap of Financial Pursuits

In modern society, money has become the ultimate marker of success, shaping priorities, decisions, and even self-worth. We're conditioned to believe that financial achievement will provide happiness, security, and freedom. But what if this pursuit is another symptom of unconscious patterns keeping people stuck?

Many people fall into the trap of thinking, *"When I have enough, I'll be happy."* But enough never comes—because it's not the money itself they seek but what they believe it will give them: validation, acceptance, or freedom from fear.

Alex's story is an example. He pours his energy into climbing the corporate ladder, convinced that reaching a certain income will bring him peace. But each new milestone leaves him just as restless as before. Rachel's pursuit takes another form—she believes the right relationship will complete her. But no matter how much love she finds, the emptiness returns.

Financial success—and any other external achievement—can't heal inner wounds. As long as we look for fulfillment outside ourselves, the cycle of striving and dissatisfaction will continue. Transformation begins when we stop chasing and start aligning our actions with personal values, using money as a tool to support who we are becoming rather than defining us.

Why Transformation?

If you've picked up this book, it's because you're ready for something more—something deeper than surface-level change. Real transformation isn't about adopting new habits or setting better goals. It's about going beneath the surface to uncover the unconscious beliefs and patterns that shape your life and rewriting those stories from the inside out.

Each chapter of this book will guide you on this journey—offering practical tools and insights to help you move forward. But beyond tools, it invites you to unlearn the false stories you've been told and reconnect with the truth of who you are.

The Role of Trauma and Healing

Trauma is often misunderstood. It's not just the big events that leave scars. Trauma can be subtle—like the belief that you're unworthy of love or the fear that being yourself will lead to rejection. These deep-seated wounds shape what you believe you deserve in life and create cycles of self-sabotage that hold you back from your true potential.

Healing isn't about fixing what's wrong—it's about gently uncovering the layers of misunderstanding that have kept you disconnected from your power. This book provides a path for long-term change—the kind that allows you to live from a place of wholeness and authenticity.

Breaking Free from the Trance

Imagine waking up every day with a clear sense of purpose, feeling aligned with your goals and grounded in who you truly are. This transformation is about waking up from the trance of conditioning, shedding old beliefs, and stepping into the freedom of being fully yourself.

Each chapter will take you deeper into this journey—from mastering your mindset to building emotional resilience, from improving communication to enhancing creativity and leadership. This isn't just a book—it's a guide to reconnecting with your authentic self and creating a life that reflects your highest potential.

Most of what's available today focuses on treating symptoms rather than addressing root causes. We're told to think positive, set better goals, or increase productivity. But real transformation requires going deeper—into the beliefs and patterns that keep you trapped.

This book offers a different path. It will help you confront limiting beliefs, release old stories, and reconnect with your true self through practical tools and soul-stirring stories like those of Alex and Rachel.

The Call to Awaken: Your Hero's Journey

You are standing at the beginning of your hero's journey—a path of awakening and reclaiming your power. Like the mythical heroes we admire, this journey requires you to step out of your comfort zone and confront the obstacles within.

Transformation isn't about becoming someone new—it's about remembering who you've always been. This book will guide you through each step, from building resilience to mastering self-discipline, helping you align your actions with your purpose in a world that constantly pulls your attention away.

Transformation isn't linear, nor does it happen overnight. Old patterns will resurface, and you'll face moments where giving up seems easier. But just like Alex and Rachel, each step forward brings you closer to living a life built on authenticity, not external expectations.

This journey is about awakening to who you are and learning to live from that place of truth. It's not about striving for perfection — it's about coming home to yourself, moment by moment, step by step.

What This Book Offers is a roadmap for transformation. It will guide you through the process of awakening. Each chapter will take you deeper into the journey — exploring the mindsets, skills, and tools needed to transform your life from the inside out.

Chapter 1: Understanding Your Inner Drive
Chapter 2: Cultivating a Growth Mindset
Chapter 3: Mastering Self-Discipline
Chapter 4: Emotional Intelligence and Success
Chapter 5: Living with Purpose and Inspiration
Chapter 6: The Art of Transformation
Chapter 7: Building Resilience
Chapter 8: The Art of Decision Making
Chapter 9: Nurturing Creativity and Innovation
Chapter 10: Leadership and Influence
Chapter 11: Achieving Work-Life Balance
Chapter 12: Financial Wellbeing and Success
Chapter 13: The Journey of Continuous Learning
Chapter 14: The Digital Age and Personal Growth
Chapter 15: Envisioning and Realizing Your Future

Yes, challenges will arise, but growth begins in those moments of discomfort. Every time you lean into fear, let go of old identities, or push through doubt, you peel away another layer of the trance and move closer to freedom.

"The privilege of a lifetime is to become who you truly are."
— Carl Jung

Are you ready to awaken? Your journey begins now.

Chapter 1: Understanding Your Inner Drive

Section 1: The Search for Purpose – Why Many Feel Lost

Marcus had always been a runner. From high school competitions to marathons in his 30s, running was more than a hobby—it was his identity. Every victory gave him a sense of achievement, and every loss felt like a personal failure. He lived for the finish line, believing that crossing it first was the only thing that mattered. But over time, something shifted. The victories felt hollow, the celebrations brief, and the satisfaction fleeting.

No matter how hard he trained, Marcus couldn't shake the sense that something was missing. He ran farther and faster, hoping the next race would reignite the spark. But with each mile, the emptiness grew. It was as if he was chasing a finish line that kept moving farther away.

The Moment of Clarity
During a particularly grueling marathon, Marcus reached a breaking point. At mile 18, exhaustion hit him like a wave. His muscles screamed, his lungs burned, and every step felt impossible. But instead of quitting or forcing himself onward, Marcus slowed to a near walk. And in that moment of stillness, a memory surfaced—his father cheering him on at one of his first races. His father had passed away years ago, but the memory was vivid. Marcus realized that his drive to win had never been just about running. It had been a way to outrun the grief he hadn't processed.

With tears in his eyes and his body on the verge of collapse, Marcus stopped chasing the victory. He decided, instead, to run for the joy of movement and as a tribute to his father's memory. He crossed the finish line hours behind his usual time, but for the first time in years, he felt at peace. It wasn't the victory that mattered—it was the meaning behind the journey.

Why We Feel Lost
Marcus's story is a reminder that many of us pursue external achievements in search of internal fulfillment, only to discover that success doesn't bring the peace we imagined. It's common to follow paths we think will make us happy—career milestones, relationships, financial goals—only to realize that even when we achieve them, a quiet dissatisfaction remains.

This disconnection often stems from chasing goals that don't align with who we truly are. Society teaches us to pursue money, recognition, and status as if they are the keys to happiness. But when we reach those milestones, the satisfaction is short-lived.

We end up stuck in a loop, chasing the next achievement, hoping it will finally bring us what we're looking for.

Alex's Story: Chasing What Doesn't Matter
Alex's life looked perfect on the outside. He had a great job, a steady income, and the respect of his colleagues. But the deeper he went into his career, the more restless he became. Each promotion felt like an empty trophy—impressive on the outside, but meaningless inside.

"Life is never made unbearable by circumstances, but only by lack of meaning and purpose." —Viktor Frankl

Alex's relentless pursuit of success wasn't driven by passion or purpose—it was driven by the need for validation. He was climbing a ladder that someone else had placed in front of him, never stopping to ask if it led to where he wanted to go. Like Marcus, Alex was running a race that wasn't truly his.

Section 2: Passion vs. Purpose – Understanding the Difference

Many people believe that passion and purpose are the same thing, but they aren't. Passion is a spark—an intense burst of excitement or enthusiasm. It's the thrill of starting a new project, the exhilaration of pursuing something you love. But passion can be fleeting, and it often comes and goes. Purpose, on the other hand, is something deeper. It's the steady force that keeps you going, even when the initial excitement wears off. Purpose sustains you through both the highs and the lows.

Why Passion Alone Isn't Enough
Relying solely on passion is like chasing fireworks. It burns

bright, but eventually, it fades, leaving you searching for the next spark. People often expect to feel passionate all the time, and when they don't, they assume they've failed or chosen the wrong path. This is a common trap—mistaking passion for purpose and becoming discouraged when the excitement inevitably wanes.

"Working hard for something we don't care about is called stress; working hard for something we love is called passion." —Simon Sinek

Purpose goes beyond the fleeting nature of passion. It's what anchors you, providing meaning and direction even when things get difficult. Purpose is the reason behind what you do—the deeper meaning that keeps you grounded, even when the road gets tough.

Discovering Your Purpose
If you've ever felt unsure of your purpose, you're not alone. Many people fall into the trap of thinking that they need to feel passionate all the time to know they are on the right path. But purpose isn't something you stumble upon—it's something you build, piece by piece, through reflection and intentional choices.

Ask yourself:

- What brings me meaning, even when it's hard?
- What would I still care about, even if no one else noticed or rewarded me?

Your purpose lies in the answers to these questions. It's not about chasing excitement, but about identifying the values and goals that pull you forward even in moments of doubt or struggle.

Rachel's Shift from Perfectionism to Purpose
For Rachel, life was all about meeting expectations—being the perfect employee, partner, and daughter. She spent years trying to excel in every area, hoping to feel validated and worthy. But no matter how much she achieved, the sense of fulfillment always slipped through her fingers.

Her breakthrough came when she asked herself, "What do I really want?" It was a simple question, but one she had avoided for years. The answer surprised her. What she truly wanted wasn't more success or recognition—it was to feel connected to herself and the people she loved. Her purpose wasn't in doing more; it was in learning to live authentically and care for herself.

The Shift from Passion to Purpose
Rachel's story highlights an important lesson: purpose isn't about doing more, it's about being aligned with what truly matters. Passion may burn brightly, but purpose gives your life direction and sustainability. Purpose allows you to keep going, even when passion flickers out.

When you stop chasing what others expect of you and start living in alignment with your values, you discover a sense of meaning that can't be shaken by external circumstances. Purpose is what sustains you through the tough moments—it's the quiet, steady force that guides you forward.

Section 3: Breaking Free from the Comfort Zone

The Comfort Zone Trap
Most people spend their lives within the boundaries of what feels familiar and safe. The comfort zone offers a sense of security, but it often becomes a cage—one that keeps you stuck in routines

that no longer serve you. Stepping outside of it feels risky, so it's easier to stay where things are predictable, even if that predictability comes at the cost of growth.

But staying in the comfort zone has a hidden price: it can slowly drain your sense of meaning and purpose. Comfort can numb you to the possibilities of change, convincing you that "good enough" is all there is.

Rachel's Story: Escaping the Pursuit of Perfection

Rachel's life was a testament to how comfort can become a trap. On the surface, everything looked perfect—she had a good job, supportive relationships, and a carefully curated life. But beneath the surface, Rachel was exhausted. Her need to be perfect in every role kept her locked in an endless cycle of doing more, achieving more, and yet feeling less fulfilled.

The perfection she chased gave her a sense of control and safety, but it also kept her from experiencing life authentically. She never allowed herself to slow down or ask what she truly wanted because perfection had become her comfort zone.

Her breakthrough came when she finally allowed herself to let go. One day, she decided to say no to an extra project at work—a small step, but a significant one. Instead of filling every minute with tasks, she spent a quiet morning reading a book, something she hadn't done in years. That moment, seemingly insignificant, sparked something inside her—a reminder of what it felt like to do something purely for joy, not approval.

Why We Stay Stuck

Rachel's experience is familiar to many. The fear of the unknown often keeps people clinging to what feels familiar, even when it no longer brings joy. The idea of stepping into something new—whether it's changing careers, ending a relationship, or simply saying no—can feel terrifying because it means leaving behind what's comfortable. But as Rachel discovered, growth requires discomfort.

Stepping out of the comfort zone isn't about taking reckless risks. It's about making intentional choices that challenge old patterns and allow you to explore new possibilities. Every time you make a small change—like Rachel's decision to prioritize self-care—you build the courage to move further beyond the boundaries of your comfort zone.

Discomfort as a Gateway to Growth
It's easy to believe that discomfort is a sign that something is wrong. But discomfort is often a signal that you're on the verge of growth. Think of it like exercise—the first few workouts are tough, and your muscles ache, but that discomfort is a sign that you're getting stronger. The same principle applies to personal growth: the moments of discomfort are where transformation happens.

The truth is, the comfort zone is not where meaning is found. Meaning lies in the challenges, the uncertainties, and the decisions that push you toward becoming the person you were meant to be. Growth begins when you lean into discomfort and trust that the struggle is part of the process.

Section 4: The Power of Ikigai – Finding the Intersection

In Japanese culture, the concept of Ikigai offers a beautiful framework for discovering purpose. The word roughly translates to "reason for being," and it represents the point where your passions, skills, and contributions to the world align. It's not just about what makes you happy; it's about finding the deeper meaning in what you do and living in harmony with it every day.

The Four Elements of Ikigai

The essence of Ikigai lies in the intersection of four key questions:

1. What do you love? (Passion)
2. What are you good at? (Vocation)
3. What does the world need? (Mission)
4. What can you be paid for? (Profession)

Where these elements meet, you find Ikigai—a life filled with meaning, joy, and fulfillment. It's about aligning your inner values with the external world, creating a balance that sustains you over time.

Applying Ikigai in Your Life

Finding your Ikigai doesn't mean you have to quit your job or make drastic changes overnight. It begins with small steps—reflecting on what brings you joy, identifying your strengths, and exploring how you can make a meaningful contribution to the world.

Here are a few practical ways to apply Ikigai:

- Journal your interests and skills: Write down what you enjoy doing and where your talents lie.
- Identify small ways to contribute: Look for opportunities to use your strengths to help others, even in simple ways.
- Evaluate your current goals: Ask yourself if they align with what you love, what you're good at, and what the world needs.

The journey toward Ikigai is personal and gradual. It's not about perfection but about moving toward alignment, one small step at a time.

A Life of Meaning and Balance

The power of Ikigai lies in its simplicity. It reminds us that purpose isn't something to chase—it's something to build by aligning what we love with what we do. When your daily actions reflect your passions, skills, and contributions, life becomes more than a checklist of achievements. It becomes a journey filled with meaning and joy.

Marcus's Discovery of Alignment

Marcus's journey from chasing victories to running for personal meaning reflects this idea of alignment. He initially focused on external validation, pushing himself to win races because he believed they defined his worth. But when he let go of that need for approval and ran to honor his father's memory, he discovered a deeper sense of purpose. This shift aligned his passion for running with a more meaningful mission, creating his own version of Ikigai.

Section 5: Setting Meaningful Goals – Aligning with Your True Self

Goals are powerful—they give direction, structure, and a sense of accomplishment. But not all goals are created equal. Many people set goals based on what they think they should want, following external expectations rather than personal values. These "should" goals often feel hollow once achieved, leaving a lingering sense of dissatisfaction.

The Problem with "Should" Goals
When goals are driven by the need for approval or societal expectations—such as earning a promotion, buying a bigger house, or achieving a specific milestone—they often lack personal meaning. While achieving these goals may provide a brief sense of satisfaction, it doesn't last. People quickly move on to the next achievement, hoping it will bring the fulfillment they seek. But fulfillment can't come from goals that aren't aligned with who you truly are.

Rachel's Shift Toward Meaningful Goals

For years, Rachel's life was filled with "should" goals. She pursued them to meet others' expectations, not because they resonated with her true self. But as she began to unlearn her habit of perfectionism, Rachel realized her goals needed to change. She asked herself a powerful question: What do I really want?

Her new goal wasn't about achieving more—it was about prioritizing self-care and building meaningful relationships. This wasn't the kind of goal that would impress others, but it felt deeply right to her. That sense of alignment gave Rachel a new kind of motivation—one that wasn't dependent on external approval.

Discovering the 'why' behind each goal is what anchors us through uncertainty

The "Why" Behind the Goal
The key to setting meaningful goals is focusing not just on the outcome but on the deeper reason behind it. The "why" gives your efforts meaning and sustains you through the inevitable challenges. A helpful tool for uncovering the deeper reason behind your goals is the "5 Whys" exercise.

1. Start with a goal (e.g., "I want to write a book").
2. Ask yourself, "Why?"
3. Then, take your answer and ask "Why?" again.
4. Repeat this process five times to uncover the core reason behind your goal.

This exercise peels back the layers of surface-level motivations, helping you connect with the authentic meaning behind your goals.

Practical Steps for Setting Aligned Goals

Here are a few ways to ensure your goals align with your true self:

- Identify your values: List your core values—what matters most to you, such as creativity, freedom, or connection.
- Make your goals process-oriented: Focus on the daily actions needed to move toward your goal, rather than fixating on the outcome.
- Visualize your future self: Imagine what your life will look and feel like once you achieve your goal. Does it align with who you are at your core?

When your goals reflect your inner values, the process of working toward them becomes meaningful in itself. Even setbacks feel manageable because you know you are on a path that resonates with who you truly are.

Quote for Reflection
"Success is not the key to happiness. Happiness is the key to success. If you love what you are doing, you will be successful." —Albert Schweitzer

This quote beautifully captures the essence of meaningful goals. When your goals are aligned with your values, success becomes a natural byproduct—not something to chase, but something that flows from living authentically.

The journey to setting meaningful goals begins with turning inward. It's not about meeting external expectations—it's about discovering what truly matters to you and aligning your actions with that truth. When your goals reflect your inner self, you experience joy in the journey, not just the destination.

"So, what are you running toward? What's the deeper reason behind your goals? The answers lie not outside of you, but within —the real journey begins by turning inward."

Chapter 2: Cultivating a Growth Mindset

Section 1: The Power of Perspective – Shifting How You See Challenges

We all face moments when things don't go as planned—failures, disappointments, or setbacks that make us question our abilities. How we interpret these moments determines whether we stay stuck or grow. Some people see failure as proof that they're not good enough, while others view it as an opportunity to learn and improve. The way we choose to frame our experiences often makes the difference between those who thrive and those who give up.

The Role of Mindset in Success
Psychologist Carol Dweck, who introduced the concept of a growth mindset, explains that people with a fixed mindset believe their talents and abilities are predetermined and unchangeable. If they succeed, it's because they were naturally

gifted; if they fail, they assume they'll never improve. On the other hand, people with a growth mindset understand that abilities can be developed through time, effort, and persistence. Failure isn't the end—it's part of the process.

This shift in mindset is subtle but powerful. It transforms failure from a threat into a teacher. People with a growth mindset don't avoid challenges; they embrace them, knowing that every obstacle offers a chance to grow.

Failure as the Greatest Teacher
Throughout history, those who've achieved the most didn't avoid failure—they embraced it. They understood that each setback held a lesson waiting to be learned. After countless failed attempts to create the lightbulb, these words were shared::

"Many of life's failures are people who did not realize how close they were to success when they gave up." — Thomas Edison

The difference between success and stagnation often comes down to the willingness to try again. Every failure contains a seed of growth, and every setback offers a new way to look at things. A growth mindset doesn't focus on avoiding failure but on using it to become stronger and wiser.

The Sculptor and the Unfinished Statue – A Story of Growth
There was once a sculptor who dreamed of creating a masterpiece—a statue that would stand as the pinnacle of his life's work. Day after day, he worked tirelessly, chipping away at the stone. But no matter how hard he tried, the figure he imagined never emerged perfectly. Every time he thought he was close, he found a flaw and had to start over.

Frustrated, the sculptor began to doubt his abilities. "Maybe I'm just not good enough," he thought. One day, a young apprentice asked him why he kept working so hard, despite the endless setbacks. The sculptor paused and said, "I've come to realize it's not the statue that's being shaped—it's me."

The sculptor's journey wasn't just about creating a flawless work of art. It was about becoming someone patient, resilient, and unafraid of imperfection. Each mistake taught him something new—not only about his craft but also about himself. In the end, whether the statue was finished or not didn't matter. What mattered was the transformation he underwent along the way.

This story beautifully illustrates the heart of a growth mindset: It's not just about the outcome—it's about who you become in the process. Like the sculptor, we are shaped by every challenge, every setback, and every imperfect moment.

The Power of Shifting Perspective

The sculptor's journey shows us that how we view our challenges matters more than the challenges themselves. A person with a growth mindset understands that every obstacle is an opportunity to grow—not a reason to quit. They see difficulties as invitations to become stronger and more capable.

This shift in thinking can transform your experience of daily life. Instead of feeling crushed by failure or overwhelmed by setbacks, you start to see them as tools for growth. Every failed project, every rejection, and every criticism becomes a chance to learn and improve.

"Obstacles do not block the path; they are the path." —**Zen Proverb**

This perspective doesn't come naturally overnight—it requires practice. But as you begin to see setbacks through the lens of growth, you'll realize that obstacles aren't roadblocks—they are guideposts, showing you where to focus your energy and effort.

Section 2: Passion vs. Purpose – Understanding the Difference

Many people believe that passion and purpose are one and the same. It's easy to assume that if you're passionate about something, it will naturally become your life's purpose. But in reality, these two concepts are distinct. Passion is the spark—an intense feeling of excitement that drives you to pursue a goal or hobby. It energizes you in the moment, making work feel effortless. But like a flame, passion can burn out when obstacles arise, leaving you questioning your path.

Purpose, on the other hand, is deeper and more enduring. Purpose sustains you even when the initial excitement fades. It's the meaning behind what you do—the reason that pulls you forward through challenges and setbacks. While passion is fleeting, purpose provides the long-term motivation needed to persevere.

The Trap of Chasing Passion
Many people struggle with the idea that they should always feel passionate about their work. When the excitement isn't constant, they assume they've chosen the wrong path. But this mindset can lead to frustration, causing people to abandon meaningful pursuits the moment things get difficult.

"Effort without meaning is just exhaustion." —Brené Brown

When passion alone drives you, setbacks feel discouraging, and motivation dwindles. But when your efforts are rooted in purpose, challenges become part of the journey rather than barriers to success. Purpose helps you push through the tough moments, providing a sense of meaning even when the spark of passion fades.

The Balance of Passion and Purpose
The key isn't to rely solely on passion or purpose—it's to align them. Passion ignites your enthusiasm, but purpose gives it direction. When you connect what excites you with a deeper sense of meaning, you find the strength to persevere through difficulties. This alignment allows you to move forward, not just when things are easy, but especially when they are hard.

Consider an artist who loves to paint. When inspiration strikes, hours pass in a blur as the artist creates. But there are also dry spells, when the canvas remains blank, and frustration sets in. If the artist's purpose is rooted only in the thrill of painting, they might give up during these tough times. But if the artist sees their work as a way to express truth, inspire others, or connect with the world, the purpose sustains them even through the uninspired moments.

Rachel's Shift Toward Purpose
Rachel had always lived by the idea that passion should guide every decision. She pursued new projects and relationships with excitement, but each time the initial spark faded, she found herself searching for the next thing. Over time, she realized that relying on passion alone wasn't enough—she needed something deeper to carry her through the inevitable challenges.

Her shift came when she began asking herself a new question: "What's the bigger reason behind what I'm doing?" This simple shift in thinking helped Rachel align her actions with a sense of purpose. She discovered that her purpose wasn't about chasing excitement—it was about building meaningful connections and contributing to others in ways that mattered to her.

With this new mindset, Rachel's approach to life changed. She no longer abandoned projects the moment they became difficult. Instead, she saw challenges as opportunities to deepen her understanding and commitment. The spark of passion still fueled her, but purpose became the steady flame that guided her.

Finding Your Own Purpose
If you've ever wondered whether you're on the right path because the excitement has faded, you're not alone. The secret isn't to find a passion that never fades—it's to align your passion with a greater sense of purpose. When you know why you're doing something, you gain the strength to push through difficult times.

Here are a few ways to explore your purpose:

- Ask yourself: What activities bring me joy, even when they're difficult?
- Reflect on your values: What do I care about, even when no one is watching?
- Look beyond the outcome: How does my work contribute to the world or the people around me?

Purpose emerges from the answers to these questions. It's not something you discover overnight—it's something you cultivate through reflection and intentional choices.

Aligning Passion with Purpose
When passion and purpose align, you create a sustainable force that carries you through life's highs and lows. Passion may provide the spark, but purpose is the flame that keeps you going. It's what transforms fleeting excitement into long-term fulfillment.

As you cultivate a growth mindset, remember: Your purpose isn't something you have to chase—it's something you build, step by step, through the choices you make every day.

Section 3: Embracing Obstacles as Opportunities

Obstacles are unavoidable in life. Failure, rejection, and disappointment will always be part of the journey. But whether these moments hold us back or help us grow depends entirely on our mindset. With a growth mindset, obstacles become stepping stones instead of stumbling blocks.

The problem isn't the obstacles themselves—it's how we view them. Some people see setbacks as proof that they aren't good enough. They avoid challenges and retreat into what feels safe. But those with a growth mindset understand that failure isn't the end of the story—it's a lesson along the way.

The Sculptor's Lesson – Becoming through Challenges
The story of the sculptor and the unfinished statue reminds us that mistakes shape us more than success. Just as the sculptor realized he wasn't just carving a statue but also shaping himself through the process, we too are transformed by how we respond to life's challenges. Growth comes from effort, struggle, and persistence—not from getting everything right the first time.

In fact, those who succeed often face the most setbacks along the way. What makes them different isn't luck or talent—it's the ability to see challenges as opportunities for growth. They don't quit when things get tough. Instead, they ask: What can I learn from this? How can I improve next time?

"Fall seven times, stand up eight." —Japanese Proverb

Reframing Failure: A Practical Shift
A key component of a growth mindset is reframing failure. It's not about avoiding mistakes but about using them as a guide for improvement. Here's how you can begin shifting your perspective:

- Ask yourself: What is this experience teaching me?
- Reflect: What skills or insights can I develop by facing this obstacle?
- Adjust your approach: If this method isn't working, what can I do differently?

This shift doesn't happen overnight. It requires practice and intentional effort. But once you start reframing failure as part of the journey, you free yourself from the fear of mistakes—and in doing so, you unlock your potential to grow.

Obstacles Are Part of the Path
Obstacles don't mean you're on the wrong path. They are part of the path. Each challenge offers a chance to develop resilience, patience, and new skills. When you stop seeing difficulties as roadblocks and start viewing them as guideposts, you become unstoppable.

"Every adversity, every failure, every heartache carries with it the seed of an equal or greater benefit." —Napoleon Hill

The earlier story of the sculptor serves as a powerful reminder: Growth isn't about perfection—it's about becoming your best self through the process of learning, failing, and trying again. Obstacles are not detours; they are essential parts of the journey.

The Power of Persistence
The most important part of cultivating a growth mindset is embracing the process, not just the outcome. Just like the sculptor who chiseled away at his unfinished statue, the real masterpiece is the person you become along the way. Each setback is an invitation to go deeper, refine your approach, and move closer to your potential.

Section 4: Daily Practices to Cultivate a Growth Mindset

Cultivating a growth mindset isn't a one-time shift—it's a daily practice. Just as your muscles grow stronger with regular exercise, your mindset becomes more resilient when you intentionally nurture it over time. Incorporating small habits into your routine can reinforce the belief that learning and growth are continuous.

1. Embrace Journaling for Reflection
Journaling allows you to process challenges and setbacks by reflecting on what worked, what didn't, and what you learned. A simple prompt—*"What did I learn today?"*—can train your mind to find lessons in every experience, even the difficult ones.

2. Reframe Negative Thoughts
Negative thoughts are natural, but with practice, you can reframe

them into opportunities for growth. Instead of saying, *"I can't do this,"* try, *"I can't do this yet."* This subtle shift emphasizes the idea that abilities can develop over time.

3. Learn to Love Feedback
Feedback can feel uncomfortable, but it's one of the most valuable tools for personal growth. Train yourself to welcome feedback by asking, *"What's one thing I can improve?"* This mindset turns criticism into an opportunity to grow rather than a personal attack.

The Role of Curiosity and Lifelong Learning
A growth mindset thrives on curiosity. Instead of seeing yourself as a fixed entity, begin to view life as a constant learning process. Try new activities, take up hobbies, or read books outside of your comfort zone. Learning something new, no matter how small, reinforces the idea that growth is always possible.

"You are never too old to set another goal or to dream a new dream." —C.S. Lewis

This mindset applies to everyday life. Whether you're working through a difficult project or navigating personal relationships, approach each situation with curiosity. Ask yourself: *What can I learn from this? How can this make me better?*

Consistency Over Perfection
The key to building a growth mindset is consistency, not perfection. It's okay to have setbacks or moments of doubt, as long as you keep coming back to the process. Just as with physical fitness, your mental resilience strengthens with regular effort, even when progress seems slow.

Growth as a Daily Choice
Cultivating a growth mindset is about more than just believing in your potential—it's about actively choosing to grow each day. Through small, intentional practices, you can rewire your mind to embrace challenges, welcome feedback, and view every experience as an opportunity to improve.

Section 5: Building Resilience Through Continuous Learning

A growth mindset doesn't just thrive on success—it flourishes through resilience. Life will inevitably present moments of failure, rejection, and setbacks. But the key to personal transformation lies not in avoiding these moments, but in bouncing back stronger every time. Resilience is the bridge between where you are and where you want to be, and continuous learning strengthens that bridge.

The Power of Persistence and Adaptability
Resilience isn't about never falling—it's about learning to adapt and rise every time you do. The most successful people aren't those who avoid failure but those who embrace it as part of the journey. Every failure contains a lesson, and every setback offers an opportunity to grow.

***"Do not judge me by my successes, judge me by how many times I fell down and got back up again."* —Nelson Mandela**

Resilience requires seeing failure as a necessary part of learning, not a permanent defeat. It involves recognizing that each challenge sharpens your skills, builds your character, and moves you closer to your potential. The willingness to learn continuously allows you to face obstacles with confidence—knowing that even if things don't go as planned, you have the tools to adjust and keep moving forward.

Learning as a Lifelong Process
Resilient people see every experience as an opportunity to learn. They adopt the mindset that life is a classroom—one filled with lessons, both big and small. Whether through books, mentors, or personal experiences, they seek out knowledge not as a means to an end but as a way of life.

Continuous learning isn't about collecting knowledge for the sake of it—it's about applying what you've learned. Each lesson becomes part of your toolkit, helping you navigate challenges more effectively in the future. The more you learn, the more resilient you become, because every lesson adds another layer to your personal growth.

Resilience in Action: Rachel's Story
When Rachel shifted her mindset from perfectionism to purpose, she didn't eliminate challenges—she changed the way she responded to them. Instead of seeing setbacks as failures, Rachel began to view them as part of the process. Whenever she faced a difficult moment, she asked herself, *"What can I learn from this?"*

Over time, this small shift made a big difference. Each time Rachel encountered an obstacle, she grew more resilient. Her failures no longer defined her—they refined her. With each challenge she overcame, she became more confident in her ability to handle whatever came next.

Practical Steps to Build Resilience

Here are a few ways to develop resilience through continuous learning:

1. Develop a Growth Routine
   Incorporate daily habits like journaling, reflection, or practicing gratitude to help you process experiences and learn from them.

2. Seek Feedback Regularly
   Treat feedback as a gift—an opportunity to improve, even when it's uncomfortable to hear.

3. Celebrate Small Wins
   Every small achievement is a step forward. Recognize your progress, even when it feels insignificant.

4. Stay Curious
   Approach each day with curiosity. Ask questions, try new things, and seek new perspectives to expand your understanding.

Growth Is a Lifelong Journey
Resilience is not a destination—it's a practice. A growth mindset keeps you moving forward, even when the path is difficult or unclear. By embracing continuous learning, you build the resilience needed to thrive in any circumstance.

Every challenge, every failure, and every success is an opportunity to grow. With each lesson you learn, you become more aligned with your potential and purpose. The key is not to aim for perfection but to stay committed to the process— knowing that the journey of growth never truly ends.

"The only way to discover the limits of the possible is to go beyond them into the impossible." —Arthur C. Clarke

Chapter 3: Mastering Self-Discipline

Section 1: The Power of Small, Consistent Actions

Discipline isn't about grand, heroic acts. It's not waking up one morning and suddenly running a marathon—it's about lacing up your shoes every day, even when you don't feel like it. The real magic of self-discipline lies in small, consistent actions that accumulate over time. Think of it like a river that carves through solid rock—not because of one powerful wave, but because of its steady, unrelenting flow.

Motivation vs. Habit:
A common misconception is that discipline hinges on motivation. Motivation feels good—it surges in bursts, making you feel invincible for a moment. But like a wave, it crashes, leaving you stranded when the tide pulls away. Discipline, on the other hand, is the ability to act regardless of how you feel. It's about creating

habits that require little to no thought, guiding you forward even when motivation fades.

"We are what we repeatedly do. Excellence, then, is not an act, but a habit." —Aristotle

Imagine a writer. She doesn't produce a novel in a single, feverish night. Instead, she writes 500 words every morning before work. There are no fireworks, no instant gratification—just the quiet, consistent effort of showing up every day. And one day, without fanfare, a finished manuscript lies before her.

The Science of Momentum:
There's a principle in physics called inertia: objects in motion stay in motion. Habits work the same way. The more consistently you show up, the easier it becomes to keep going. This is the power of small wins—they generate momentum, making each subsequent action feel a little lighter.

Willpower is Finite, Systems Are Sustainable:
Willpower, like any muscle, gets fatigued over time. If you rely solely on willpower to make every decision—whether to exercise, eat healthily, or stay focused—you'll eventually burn out. This is why systems are essential. Systems automate the process, removing the need for constant decision-making.

For example:

- Want to eat healthier? Pre-plan your meals every Sunday.
- Want to save money? Automate your savings each month.

- Want to exercise more? Lay out your workout clothes the night before.

These small systems reduce friction, making discipline feel less like a struggle and more like a natural part of your day. The trick isn't to aim for perfection but consistency. Even a 1% improvement each day compounds into remarkable results over time.

Section 2: Building Lasting Habits – Aligning Discipline with Your Identity

Real, sustainable discipline emerges when habits are tied to identity rather than outcomes. Instead of focusing on what you want to achieve, shift your attention to the person you wish to become. This mindset creates a powerful internal alignment—your habits stop feeling like obligations and start becoming expressions of who you are.

The Identity Shift in Action:
Think about two people trying to quit smoking. When offered a cigarette, the first person says, "No thanks, I'm trying to quit." The second says, "No thanks, I'm not a smoker." The subtle difference is profound—the second person isn't merely resisting temptation; they're reinforcing a new identity.

This principle applies across all areas of life. When you identify as a person who exercises regularly or someone who values personal growth, your actions naturally align with that identity. It becomes less about effort and more about who you are.

Designing Your Environment to Support Discipline:
Your environment plays a key role in habit formation. Often, your

surroundings dictate your behavior more than willpower does. A cluttered desk invites distraction, while a neat workspace encourages focus. If your goal is to read more, place a book where you'll see it—on your bedside table, for example. If you want to eat healthily, fill your fridge with nutritious options and keep junk food out of sight.

"You do not rise to the level of your goals. You fall to the level of your systems." —James Clear

Aligning your environment with your identity creates effortless discipline. When your surroundings nudge you toward good habits, it's easier to stay consistent even when motivation wanes.

The Power of Micro-Habits:
Discipline isn't about building habits for the sake of habit—it's about aligning each small, intentional action with the person you aspire to become. It's about knowing that every micro-habit, no matter how small, is a reflection of the disciplined person you are becoming.

Big goals can feel daunting, leading to procrastination. But when you break those goals into tiny, manageable actions, the path becomes easier to walk. Start small—so small that it feels almost effortless:

- Want to write a book? Start by writing just 100 words a day.
- Want to meditate? Begin with a minute of deep breathing.
- Want to get fit? Start with five minutes of stretching each morning.

These micro-habits build trust with yourself. Every time you follow through, you send a message to your subconscious: *"I am someone who does what I say I'll do."* This internal trust becomes the foundation for lasting discipline. It's not about grand gestures but consistent alignment between your actions and the person you aspire to be.

Section 3: The Samurai and the Cherry Blossom Tree – A Story of Patience and Mastery

In a small village nestled between towering mountains, there lived a young samurai determined to become a master swordsman. He practiced tirelessly, rising before dawn to swing his sword until his arms ached and his body dripped with sweat. Yet despite his relentless effort, he felt as though mastery slipped further from his grasp each day. Frustration gnawed at him. He had believed that hard work would guarantee success, but the results he sought remained elusive.

One crisp spring morning, the samurai wandered into a secluded garden. There, under the canopy of a cherry blossom tree, he paused. The tree stood still and serene, its branches adorned with buds on the verge of blooming. As he sat in quiet contemplation, a petal slowly began to unfurl before his eyes. It moved neither fast nor slow but in perfect rhythm with the season's change. The tree bloomed, not in response to urgency, but in harmony with the natural flow of time.

In that tranquil moment, the samurai realized the flaw in his approach. Mastery, like the blossoming of the cherry tree, could not be forced. It was cultivated over time, one small action at a time, with patience and intention. The lesson became clear: his journey wasn't just about achieving perfection—it was about learning to embrace the process.

The young warrior returned to his training with renewed perspective. His swings became more deliberate, each movement an expression of devotion rather than frustration. He stopped chasing quick results and instead focused on mastering the fundamentals. Days turned into weeks, and weeks into seasons. Slowly but surely, progress began to reveal itself—not as a sudden breakthrough, but as subtle improvements that built upon one another.

The story of the samurai teaches us that discipline is not just about persistence—it's about patience. The cherry blossom tree does not bloom under pressure, nor does mastery appear overnight. Both unfold in their own time, nurtured by small, consistent efforts.

Discipline is not only about reaching a destination but about becoming someone who values the journey. It requires trust: trust that each action, no matter how small, carries meaning. Trust that growth, though invisible at times, is always happening beneath the surface. And most importantly, trust that when the season is right, the blossoms will appear.

The samurai learned that mastery unfolds over time, but his lesson was deeper than just patience—it taught him to trust the process, even when progress was invisible. This mirrors our own journey with discipline. Life doesn't always reward consistent effort immediately, and setbacks are inevitable. But just like the cherry blossom that blooms in its season, resilience ensures that we keep moving forward, trusting that growth is happening beneath the surface, even when we can't see it.

Section 4: Overcoming Setbacks – Staying on Track When Life Gets Hard

Even the most disciplined among us encounter setbacks. Life has a way of throwing unexpected challenges—busy schedules, health issues, emotional struggles. The key isn't to avoid setbacks, but to recover quickly. Discipline isn't about perfection; it's about persistence.

The Two-Day Rule:
A powerful strategy to maintain consistency is the *Two-Day Rule*: Never miss two days in a row. Missing one day is understandable —life happens, and sometimes we need rest. But missing two days creates a gap that's harder to bridge. If you miss a workout, skip a habit, or let something slide, the next day becomes an opportunity to course-correct. The Two-Day Rule offers flexibility without sacrificing momentum.

Setbacks often come with guilt, which can paralyze progress. But instead of dwelling on mistakes, treat them as feedback. Ask yourself:

- What triggered this lapse?
- What can I do differently next time?

This approach shifts your mindset from frustration to learning, turning setbacks into opportunities for growth.

The Role of Emotions in Discipline:
Many setbacks are emotional. Boredom, frustration, or doubt can derail even the most committed efforts. Recognizing these emotions and learning to sit with them is part of mastering discipline. Mindfulness practices—like journaling or meditation—

help you become aware of emotional patterns, giving you the tools to respond rather than react.

Winston Churchill's words ring true:
"Success is not final, failure is not fatal: It is the courage to continue that counts."

Practicing self-compassion is essential during setbacks. Discipline isn't about punishment but about treating yourself with kindness. When you view setbacks as part of the process, they become stepping stones, not stumbling blocks.

Discipline isn't about deprivation or punishment—it's a form of self-care. It's about building the kind of life that aligns with your values and brings you closer to your goals. When practiced with kindness and intention, discipline becomes a tool that empowers rather than restricts. It offers freedom—freedom from chaos, procrastination, and the stress of unfulfilled potential. Each disciplined action is an act of love toward your future self.

Section 5: Aligning Daily Habits with Long-Term Goals

Many people struggle with discipline because they focus too much on the end goal and not enough on the process. But discipline thrives when daily actions align with long-term values. Each habit, no matter how small, becomes a piece of the larger vision.

Core Values as Anchors:
Start by identifying your core values—those guiding principles that define what matters most to you. Whether it's health, creativity, connection, or growth, these values provide direction.

When your habits reflect these values, discipline becomes more sustainable.

For example:

- If health is a priority, create a habit of exercising for 10 minutes daily.
- If creativity is important, set aside 15 minutes each morning for writing or brainstorming.
- If growth matters, make a habit of reading or learning something new every day.

The "5 Whys" Technique:
To uncover the deeper motivation behind your goals, use the 5 Whys method. This involves asking yourself the question "Why?" five times, each time based on the previous answer, to get to the root of your goal. For example, if your goal is to get fit, you might follow this process:

1. Why do I want to get fit?
Because I want to feel healthier.

2. Why do I want to feel healthier?
Because I want more energy.

3. Why do I want more energy?
So I can be more present for my family.

4. Why do I want to be more present for my family?
Because I value spending quality time with them.

5. Why is spending quality time with my family important?
Because it brings me joy and strengthens our bond.

By using the 5 Whys technique, you can discover the deeper values that drive your goals, helping to ensure that your discipline is rooted in meaningful purpose.

Discipline as a Way of Being:
When your actions align with your values, discipline transforms from a struggle into a natural way of being. It's no longer about forcing yourself to do things—it becomes about living in harmony with the person you aspire to be. Daily habits aren't chores; they're expressions of your identity and your future self.

Discipline isn't about reaching the finish line—it's about becoming someone who honors their commitments, not just to others, but to themselves. When discipline flows from identity, the journey itself becomes the reward.

Chapter 4: Emotional Intelligence and Success

Section 1: Understanding the Layers of Emotional Intelligence

Think about the last time you felt frustrated—maybe a friend canceled plans at the last minute, or someone cut you off in traffic. Did you react immediately, or did you take a moment to process what you were feeling? Emotional intelligence starts with those small moments, where you decide whether to react or respond.

At its heart, emotional intelligence isn't about mastering emotions like a robot—it's about becoming more aware of what's happening inside you and learning how to work with it. It's recognizing, "Ah, I'm angry right now," without letting that anger control your next move. It's also noticing when someone else is feeling down and knowing how to respond in a way that makes them feel seen and understood.

Psychologists have mapped out different layers of emotional intelligence—self-awareness, self-regulation, motivation, empathy, and social skills. But you don't need to remember all those terms to understand it. The essence of emotional intelligence is about knowing yourself well enough to steer your emotions rather than letting them steer you.

It's like being the captain of a boat on a stormy sea. You can't control the waves, but you can decide how you're going to navigate them. Are you going to steer right into them, hoping brute force will keep you afloat? Or are you going to adjust your sails, find your balance, and ride the waves with skill?

Developing emotional intelligence is a lot like that—it's about practicing small adjustments every day. Maybe it's catching yourself before snapping at a coworker or giving yourself five minutes to breathe when you feel overwhelmed. Over time, these small adjustments become second nature.

Here's the thing: emotional intelligence isn't about suppressing emotions. It's about engaging with them intentionally, using them as signposts rather than roadblocks. Every feeling—anger, joy, frustration, excitement—has something to tell you about what matters most to you. The more you tune in, the more aligned your actions become with your values and goals.

And when you start seeing emotions as allies rather than enemies, personal growth becomes a whole lot easier. You'll stop seeing setbacks as failures and start seeing them as part of the journey. It's in those moments—when you pause, reflect, and choose your response—that real growth happens.

Section 2: The Power of Emotional Awareness and Self-Regulation

We've all had those moments where emotions sneak up on us out of nowhere. Maybe you were having a good day until someone said something that hit a nerve—and suddenly, frustration or anger takes over. Emotional awareness is about catching those moments before they spiral, like noticing the first drops of rain before a storm rolls in. It's not about shutting down your feelings but recognizing what's happening in the moment.

Self-regulation, on the other hand, is the art of choosing how to respond once you become aware of your emotions. Imagine it like this: emotions are visitors knocking on your door. Some show up unannounced, and not all are welcome. But self-regulation gives you the power to decide which visitors get to stay, and for how long.

Think about a heated argument with someone close to you. In the heat of the moment, it's easy to say something you'll regret—something that can't be unsaid. Emotional regulation is like pausing before you speak, giving yourself the space to respond thoughtfully instead of reacting impulsively. It's not about bottling up your emotions but about channeling them in a way that serves you and the relationship.

Why This Matters for Personal Growth
When you can regulate your emotions, setbacks stop feeling like disasters. Instead of getting stuck in frustration, you can say, "Okay, that didn't go as planned—what can I learn from it?" This

mindset shift allows you to keep moving forward, even when life throws you curveballs. The ability to pause, reflect, and course-correct in difficult moments is what separates growth from stagnation.

Self-awareness and self-regulation work together like a well-tuned engine. One without the other doesn't get you very far. If you're aware of your emotions but can't regulate them, you'll feel stuck in cycles of frustration. If you're trying to regulate without awareness, it's like driving blindfolded—you're bound to crash sooner or later.

Here's a practical exercise:
Next time you feel overwhelmed, pause and name the emotion you're experiencing—out loud if you can. There's something powerful about labeling your feelings: "I feel anxious" or "I feel disappointed." It might seem simple, but naming emotions takes away some of their power. It shifts them from something overwhelming into something manageable.

And if you want to take it a step further, ask yourself: "What do I need right now?" Sometimes the answer will be rest, a conversation, or even a moment of stillness. The more you practice this, the better you become at recognizing what your emotions are asking from you.

At its core, self-regulation is a way of staying aligned with your goals and values, even when emotions run high. It doesn't mean you won't feel upset, frustrated, or discouraged—it means those emotions won't drive the bus. You'll still be in control, steering your life where you want it to go.

Just as self-regulation deepens your control over your emotions, empathy expands your ability to understand and connect with others.

Section 3: Building Empathy – Connecting with Others on a Deeper Level

Empathy is often misunderstood as simply putting yourself in someone else's shoes. But it's more than that—it's about truly *feeling* what another person is experiencing, even if their situation or emotions are different from your own. It's the ability to listen beyond words, sensing the emotions that lie underneath someone's silence, frustration, or joy.

The truth is, everyone is carrying something—worries, hopes, regrets, or dreams. When you develop empathy, you begin to see beyond surface interactions. That friend who snapped at you may not be angry with you at all—maybe they're overwhelmed with stress. The person who seems distant might just be battling emotions they don't know how to express. Empathy allows you to recognize the humanity in others, fostering connection rather than judgment.

The Shift from "Me" to "We"

In today's fast-paced world, it's easy to get wrapped up in our own problems and priorities. But empathy reminds us to shift from *me* to *we*. It's about being fully present when someone is speaking—listening not to respond, but to understand. In those moments, empathy becomes a bridge that connects people, creating deeper, more meaningful relationships.

Here's a story:
A man was rushing through an airport, late for his flight. As he hurried toward the gate, he accidentally bumped into a young boy, knocking his bag to the ground. Frustrated, the man started to move on without a word. But something made him stop. He looked back and saw the boy scrambling to pick up his belongings—an old, torn jacket, a few coins, and a worn-out book. His hands fumbled with the torn jacket, a hint of fear in his eyes, as if the world had already given him too much to carry.

In that instant, the man's frustration melted away. He knelt to help the boy and asked, "Are you okay?" The boy looked up, surprised, and gave a small nod. It was a brief exchange, but in that moment, the man realized something profound: the world slows down when we choose empathy. That small act of kindness—pausing, noticing, and helping—made all the difference for both of them.

The Impact of Empathy on Growth
Empathy isn't just about being kind—it's a skill that accelerates personal growth. When you understand others more deeply, you also begin to understand yourself. You recognize the emotions, fears, and needs that connect all people, allowing you to navigate relationships with more grace and patience.

Empathy also teaches you how to respond thoughtfully rather than react emotionally. It strengthens your relationships because people feel seen and understood, which builds trust over time. And trust is the foundation of every meaningful connection—whether personal or professional.

Developing empathy takes practice. Start with small moments:

- Pause before judging: When someone behaves in a way that frustrates you, ask yourself, "What might they be going through?"
- Listen without interrupting: In conversations, practice active listening—focusing entirely on the other person without planning your response.
- Check in with others: A simple "How are you, really?" can open the door to deeper conversations.

Empathy isn't about always getting it right; it's about showing up with an open heart, ready to understand. And the more you practice it, the more natural it becomes—not just as a skill, but as a way of being.

Section 4: Navigating Emotional Triggers and Maintaining Resilience

We all have emotional triggers—those moments when something hits us unexpectedly, stirring up intense feelings like anger, fear, or sadness. Maybe it's a criticism from a coworker that reminds you of past failures, or a comment from a loved one that stings more than it should. Triggers are powerful because they tap into unresolved emotions, often catching us off guard.

Navigating emotional triggers isn't about avoiding them—it's about learning to respond with awareness rather than react impulsively. Think of it like surfing: you can't stop the waves, but you can learn to ride them. It's not easy, but with practice, you develop emotional resilience—the ability to stay grounded even when emotions threaten to pull you under.

Spotting Triggers Before They Take Over
The first step to navigating triggers is recognizing them as they

arise. Pay attention to your body's signals—tightness in the chest, a clenched jaw, or racing thoughts. These physical cues are often the first sign that something has touched a nerve. When you notice these signals early, you can create space between the trigger and your reaction.

Here's a simple but powerful technique: Name it to tame it. When you feel triggered, pause and say to yourself, "I feel angry" or "I feel hurt." Naming the emotion helps you step back from it, giving you the clarity to choose your next move.

Responding with Resilience
Resilience isn't about suppressing emotions or pretending you're unaffected. It's about feeling your emotions fully without letting them dictate your actions. A helpful way to practice this is through reframing—shifting your perspective on the situation. For example, instead of thinking, "They're trying to hurt me," you might reframe it as, "They might be having a bad day." Reframing doesn't change the facts, but it helps you respond from a place of understanding rather than anger.

Another technique for building resilience is the three-breath practice. When you feel overwhelmed, take three slow, deep breaths. Inhale through your nose, hold for a moment, and exhale slowly through your mouth. With each breath, imagine releasing tension from your body and clearing your mind. This simple practice brings you back to the present moment, grounding you before you respond.

Turning Triggers into Teachers
Every emotional trigger offers an opportunity for growth. Ask yourself, "What is this reaction trying to tell me?" Often, triggers point to unresolved emotions or unmet needs. Maybe a harsh

comment from someone triggers your fear of failure, or a distant partner stirs up old feelings of abandonment. These moments can be difficult, but they also offer a chance to understand yourself on a deeper level.

Here's the key: resilience doesn't mean never getting triggered. It means knowing how to recover quickly when you do. Each time you catch yourself before reacting, you build emotional strength. And over time, triggers lose their grip on you, allowing you to move through life with more ease and grace.

Section 5: Aligning Emotions with Personal Values and Long-Term Goals

Emotions can be tricky—they ebb and flow, sometimes pulling us in directions that feel disconnected from what we truly want. One day you might feel fired up about a goal, ready to give it everything, and the next day, doubt or frustration creeps in. This is where emotional intelligence meets long-term success. It's not about forcing yourself to feel positive all the time but learning how to align your emotions with the values and goals that matter most to you.

The Role of Values as Emotional Anchors

When emotions run high—whether from stress, excitement, or setbacks—values serve as anchors that keep you grounded. Think of values like a compass, pointing you toward the life you want to build. If creativity, health, or connection are part of your core values, your emotions become signals to let you know if you're aligned or drifting off course.

For example, if you feel anxious every time you neglect your creative projects, it's likely because creativity is central to your sense of fulfillment. Recognizing this allows you to recalibrate—returning to actions that reflect your values. In this way, emotions act like signposts, guiding you back toward what matters.

A friend of mine found herself disconnected from her passion for art after starting a demanding job. When anxiety crept in, she realized her value of creativity was being neglected. Scheduling even 15 minutes of daily drawing became her lifeline back to emotional balance.

Turning Values into Daily Practices
Alignment isn't just about identifying your values—it's about living them. A lot of people set ambitious goals, only to lose motivation along the way because their day-to-day actions aren't aligned with what they truly care about. The trick is to break down big goals into small, meaningful habits that reflect your values every day.

- If health is important: Build a habit of taking a daily walk, even if it's just 10 minutes.
- If personal growth matters: Commit to reading one chapter of a book every evening.
- If connection is key: Make it a habit to call or message a friend once a week.

These small actions create emotional consistency. Even when motivation dips, these habits remind you of who you are and what you value. Over time, alignment between emotions, values, and actions becomes second nature.

Creating an Emotional Feedback Loop
One of the most powerful things you can do is create an emotional feedback loop—where emotions, actions, and values reinforce each other. Here's how it works:

1. Feel: Tune into your emotions and notice what they're telling you.
2. Align: Adjust your actions so they reflect your core values.
3. Act: Take small, consistent steps toward your long-term goals.

Each time you take action that aligns with your values, it creates a sense of accomplishment and emotional fulfillment. This feedback loop strengthens your discipline and builds trust with yourself.

The Freedom of Alignment

When your emotions, values, and goals are in harmony, discipline stops feeling like a chore. It becomes a natural expression of who you are. This alignment also creates freedom—freedom from the mental clutter that comes with conflicting emotions and misplaced priorities. Instead of feeling pulled in different directions, you move forward with clarity, knowing that every step you take is aligned with the life you want to create.

Chapter 5: Living with Purpose and Inspiration

Section 1: Discovering Purpose – The Compass for Your Journey

"He who has a why to live can bear almost any how." — Friedrich Nietzsche

We all have moments where life feels scattered—like we're pulled in a hundred different directions, unsure where to focus. In those moments, it's easy to get lost in the noise and feel disconnected from what matters most. This is where purpose steps in. Purpose isn't just some lofty ideal or grand mission reserved for a lucky few. It's the personal meaning you give to your actions—something that makes even the smallest effort feel worthwhile.

Think of purpose like a compass. Just as a compass points north, your purpose provides direction when the road ahead isn't clear. It helps you cut through distractions and focus on what matters. Without it, even the most talented and disciplined person can feel stuck, moving through life without a sense of meaning.

Purpose isn't always obvious. It doesn't arrive in a sudden flash of insight. Sometimes, it unfolds over time—like a slow-burning flame that grows brighter the more you nurture it. And sometimes, it shows up in unexpected ways: in a conversation with a friend, in a hobby you didn't realize you loved, or in the challenges that force you to grow.

The Role of Curiosity in Finding Purpose
Curiosity is often the first step toward discovering purpose. It's like following a trail of breadcrumbs—each small spark of curiosity leading you closer to something meaningful. Maybe you've always been curious about storytelling, entrepreneurship, or helping others. Following those sparks, even if they seem small, can open doors to new experiences and insights you didn't know existed.

The Intersection of Passion and Contribution
A sense of purpose often lies at the intersection of what lights you up and how you can contribute to others. It's not just about doing what you love but finding ways to make an impact. When you align your passions with service—whether that's through your work, relationships, or personal projects—you create a deeper connection to your purpose.

Finding purpose isn't about having everything figured out. It's about taking small steps every day toward what feels meaningful, trusting that the path will reveal itself as you move forward. Purpose isn't a destination—it's a way of traveling through life with clarity, even when the road gets rough.

Section 2: Aligning Purpose with Daily Actions

Having a sense of purpose is powerful, but purpose alone isn't enough. The real challenge lies in bringing that purpose into your everyday life—through the habits you build, the small choices you make, and the goals you pursue. Purpose isn't just an abstract ideal; it becomes real when it shows up in how you move through each day. This is where purpose and motivation intersect—because when your purpose aligns with your actions, motivation flows more naturally, even on tough days.

How Purpose Fuels Sustainable Motivation
When your purpose aligns with your actions, motivation flows more naturally. Motivation alone isn't enough—it has to be connected to something meaningful. As Tony Robbins says.. *'People are not lazy. They simply have impotent goals—that is, goals that do not inspire them.'* With purpose as your guide, even the hardest days feel more manageable.

Purpose creates a sense of internal alignment—it connects your values with your actions, giving meaning to every step, no matter how small. Motivation, on the other hand, is like the energy that powers you forward. While motivation may fade at times, purpose remains steady, acting as a deeper source of fuel when the journey becomes challenging.

For example, an athlete who views training as part of a greater mission to inspire others will push through the difficult days because their effort is tied to a meaningful purpose. This alignment between purpose and action ensures that even when motivation dips, you have a reason to keep going—because the path itself carries value, not just the result.

The Role of Small, Daily Actions in Alignment
The key is to align small, everyday actions with your larger sense of purpose. Even the tiniest decisions—like how you start your morning or how you treat a stranger—can reflect your purpose. If helping others is central to your purpose, something as simple as a kind word to a colleague becomes a meaningful act. If creativity is part of who you are, even five minutes spent brainstorming each day keeps you connected to that value.

Creating a Feedback Loop Between Purpose and Progress
When your purpose and actions are aligned, it creates an emotional feedback loop—where small wins reinforce your sense of meaning, and that sense of meaning fuels your motivation.

1. **Clarify your purpose:** Be clear about the deeper reason behind your actions.
2. **Set achievable goals:** Break your purpose into bite-sized tasks that provide quick wins.
3. **Celebrate progress:** Acknowledge each milestone, no matter how small, to keep yourself motivated.

This feedback loop ensures that every step forward strengthens both your motivation and your sense of purpose. Even on the hard days, you'll know that your actions are aligned with the person you want to be and the life you want to create.

The Freedom of Alignment
When your emotions, values, and goals are aligned, discipline and motivation stop feeling like chores. Instead, they become natural expressions of who you are. This alignment creates

freedom—freedom from mental clutter and the stress of feeling pulled in different directions. With purpose as your guide, you'll move forward with clarity, knowing that even the smallest actions are part of something bigger.

Having a sense of purpose is powerful, but purpose alone isn't enough. The real challenge lies in bringing that purpose into your everyday life—into the choices you make and the habits you build. It's easy to talk about purpose in grand terms, but it only becomes real when it's reflected in your daily actions.

Think of purpose like a thread running through the fabric of your life. Each day, you weave that thread through the choices you make. Some days, it might feel easy—like when you're working on something that excites you or spending time with people who uplift you. But other days, the thread might seem harder to grasp—when routine feels dull, or setbacks test your patience.

Micro-Actions Build Alignment
The key is to align small, everyday actions with your larger sense of purpose. Even the tiniest decisions—like how you start your morning or how you treat a stranger—can reflect your purpose. If your purpose involves helping others, for example, something as simple as a kind gesture toward a colleague aligns with that purpose. If creativity is central to your life, spending five minutes sketching or brainstorming ideas each day keeps you connected to what matters.

Purpose doesn't require sweeping changes. It's about finding small ways to express your values, no matter how ordinary the day seems.

Purpose as a Lifeline During Setbacks
When things get tough, purpose acts as a lifeline. It reminds you that even the hardest moments have meaning—that struggles and challenges aren't just obstacles but part of the journey. People who live with purpose often find that setbacks don't derail them as easily because they have a clear sense of *why* they keep going. It's not just about achieving goals—it's about moving in a direction that feels meaningful, even when progress is slow.

The Power of Rituals in Purposeful Living
One way to stay connected to your purpose is through rituals—small, intentional practices that reinforce your values. For example:

- A morning walk to reflect on your goals.
- A weekly check-in with yourself to assess how aligned you are with your purpose.
- A gratitude journal to remind yourself of the progress you've made, even in tough times.

These rituals become touchpoints, grounding you when life feels overwhelming and helping you stay aligned with what matters most. Over time, these practices create a sense of flow—where purpose and action merge, and life feels more intentional.

Just as aligning purpose with daily actions creates clarity, staying connected to your purpose becomes essential when life throws unexpected challenges your way.

Section 3: Purpose as a Guide Through Challenges and Uncertainty

Life has a way of throwing unexpected challenges our way—setbacks, moments of doubt, and seasons of uncertainty. In these moments, purpose becomes more than just a nice idea—it becomes your compass, helping you navigate through life's storms. When everything feels chaotic or unclear, having a clear sense of purpose keeps you grounded. It reminds you that even when the path isn't straight, you're still moving in the right direction.

The Lighthouse Effect
Think of purpose like a lighthouse. When the sea is calm, the lighthouse may seem unnecessary—it's just there in the background. But when the storm hits, and you lose sight of the shore, that steady beam of light becomes essential. Purpose works the same way. It doesn't eliminate obstacles, but it gives you something to aim for when things get tough. It reminds you that even if today feels overwhelming, you're still on a meaningful path.

Staying Committed When Doubt Creeps In
Challenges often stir up doubt, making you question whether the effort is even worth it. In those moments, it's easy to lose sight of your purpose and fall into the trap of second-guessing yourself. But doubt is not a sign that you're off course—it's often a sign that you're growing. Purpose gives you the courage to keep moving forward, even when the outcome isn't guaranteed.

Here's a practice: When doubt arises, revisit the *why* behind your efforts. Ask yourself, *What drew me to this path in the first place? What difference do I want to make?* Sometimes, reconnecting with the original spark of purpose is enough to reignite your motivation.

How Purpose Transforms Failure into Growth
One of the most powerful things about purpose is how it changes your relationship with failure. When you're connected to your purpose, failure stops being the end of the road—it becomes part of the process. Every setback becomes a lesson, every misstep a teacher. Instead of seeing failure as proof that you're not good enough, you start seeing it as feedback, guiding you toward the next step.

Consider this: When a sailor encounters rough waters, they don't abandon the journey—they adjust their sails and keep going. Purpose gives you the same ability to course-correct. It allows you to embrace the detours and challenges as part of the journey, rather than obstacles that derail you.

Purpose Provides Meaning, Even When Success Is Unclear
Not every step on the journey will come with a clear reward. Sometimes, you'll put in effort without immediate results. This is where purpose becomes essential—it provides meaning, even in the absence of success. Purpose gives you the strength to continue, trusting that your actions are building toward something greater, even if the outcome isn't visible yet.

At the end of the day, purpose isn't just about reaching a destination. It's about how you show up along the way. It's what keeps you moving when the journey is difficult, what makes even the smallest progress feel significant, and what helps you find meaning even when things don't go as planned.

Section 4: The Ripple Effect of Purpose – How Your Actions Impact Others

Purpose isn't just a personal journey; it creates ripples that extend far beyond yourself. Every action driven by purpose influences the people around you—sometimes in ways you may never see. When you live with intention, the way you show up, the choices you make, and the energy you bring to your relationships all contribute to the world around you. Purpose is contagious; it inspires others to find meaning in their own lives.

Small Acts, Big Impact
You don't have to change the world to make a difference. A simple conversation with a friend, a thoughtful gesture toward a stranger, or a word of encouragement to a colleague can spark something powerful. Purpose is about showing up fully, even in the smallest moments, knowing that your actions have the potential to create lasting effects.

Think of a teacher who spends years pouring energy into students. Some of those students might never express their gratitude, and the teacher may never see the full impact of her work. Yet decades later, those same students might go on to make meaningful contributions to society—contributions that are, in part, a reflection of the teacher's influence. Purpose works like that: the ripples of your efforts travel further than you might ever know.

Years later, one of those students might become a doctor, treating patients with the same compassion that teacher modeled—unaware that her influence planted the seed for that kindness.

Inspiring Others Through Purposeful Living
When you align your actions with your purpose, people around you notice. You inspire others—not by preaching, but by living in

a way that reflects your values. Purposeful living is magnetic; it draws people in and encourages them to reflect on their own lives. Whether you realize it or not, your example can ignite change in others, creating a ripple effect of positivity and meaning.

It's not about trying to be perfect. Purposeful living is about being authentic—embracing both your strengths and imperfections and showing others that it's okay to grow along the way. This authenticity creates deeper connections and fosters trust, both in personal and professional relationships.

Purpose as a Legacy
Living with purpose is about more than achieving goals—it's about the person you become along the way. Or, as

Henry David Thoreau said: *'What you get by achieving your goals is not as important as what you become by achieving your goals."* Every small step taken with intention shapes your future self.

One of the most beautiful aspects of purpose is that it outlives you. The values you live by, the kindness you show, and the contributions you make become part of your legacy. You may never know the full extent of the impact you've had, but that doesn't diminish its significance. Purposeful actions, no matter how small, create ripples that continue to influence others long after you're gone.

Purpose isn't just about what you achieve—it's about who you become along the way and how your presence shapes the world. When you align your life with your purpose, you create a legacy that transcends accomplishments. You leave behind more than just a list of achievements—you leave behind a life well-lived.

Section 5: Purpose and Flow – Living in Alignment with Your Why

"The best moments in our lives are not the passive, receptive, relaxing times... The best moments usually occur if a person's body or mind is stretched to its limits in a voluntary effort to accomplish something difficult and worthwhile." —Mihaly Csikszentmihalyi

When purpose aligns with action, you enter a state known as flow—those moments where time seems to disappear, and you feel fully immersed in what you're doing. It's not that the tasks are easy, but they feel meaningful, engaging your full attention without resistance. Flow occurs when the challenge matches your skills and aligns with your values, creating a sense of effortless productivity.

How Flow Reinforces Purpose

Flow states are a sign that you're on the right track—that your daily actions resonate with your purpose. When you experience flow, you know that what you're doing matters, even if the rewards aren't immediate. This feeling creates emotional resilience, making it easier to stay motivated through challenges.

Flow as a Feedback Loop

When your purpose creates flow, the experience itself becomes the reward. This reinforces your sense of meaning and keeps you moving forward, even when setbacks occur. Flow helps you stay present—focusing not on the result but on the joy of the process itself.

Practical Tips for Cultivating Flow:

- Identify tasks that stretch but don't overwhelm you: Flow happens when tasks are challenging enough to engage you without causing frustration.
- Minimize distractions: Flow requires deep focus—find time and space to engage fully with meaningful activities.
- Take breaks to recharge: Rest is part of the process. Even purposeful living requires time to reflect and recover.

Living in alignment with your purpose brings ease to even the most difficult tasks. You'll find that life feels less like a series of obstacles and more like a journey worth taking—where every moment contributes to something greater than yourself.

Chapter 6: The Art of Transformation

Section 1: Change as a Natural Part of Life

"The only way to make sense out of change is to plunge into it, move with it, and join the dance." —Alan Watts

Life is always changing—whether we like it or not. Seasons shift, relationships evolve, and circumstances we once thought were permanent eventually pass. The truth is, change is the only constant in life. But even though we know this intellectually, embracing change can still feel uncomfortable. It's human nature to resist uncertainty and cling to what feels familiar, even when the familiar no longer serves us.
Transformation begins with accepting that change is not the enemy—it's part of the rhythm of life. Just as trees shed their leaves in the fall to make way for new growth in the spring, we,

too, must release what no longer serves us to create space for something new. The process isn't always easy. It requires trust—trust in the unknown, trust in yourself, and trust that the discomfort of change is part of the transformation.

Learning to Let Go
One of the most challenging aspects of transformation is letting go—whether it's an outdated belief, an unfulfilling habit, or even a relationship that no longer aligns with who you are becoming. Letting go can feel like a loss, but it's also an opportunity to grow. Each time you release something that's holding you back, you create space for something new to enter your life.

Think about a caterpillar. It doesn't become a butterfly by holding on to the safety of its cocoon. It transforms by surrendering to the process, trusting that the wings it needs will grow in time. The same is true for us—real transformation happens when we're willing to step out of our comfort zones and trust the process, even when we can't see the full picture yet.

Discomfort as a Sign of Growth
The discomfort that comes with change isn't a sign that something is wrong—it's a sign that you're growing. Growth and comfort cannot coexist. If you're feeling stretched, challenged, or even uncertain, it likely means you're on the right path.
Embracing this discomfort is what allows transformation to unfold.

Here's a mindset shift: Instead of fearing discomfort, start seeing it as a sign of progress. Each time you push through discomfort, you expand your capacity to handle change. Transformation isn't just about reaching a new destination—it's about becoming someone who can navigate life's ups and downs with resilience and grace.

Embracing change is the first step, but the real magic happens when you learn to see challenges not as obstacles but as opportunities for growth.

Section 2: The Mindset Shift – From Problems to Possibilities

Transformation isn't just about changing your circumstances—it's about changing the way you see the world. The biggest obstacle to transformation isn't the challenges themselves but the way we interpret them. Many of us look at obstacles and think, *Why is this happening to me?* But transformation begins when you shift that mindset to: *What is this teaching me?* or *How can I grow through this?*

The Power of Reframing Challenges

Reframing is a powerful tool for transformation. It's the art of looking at a situation from a different angle, finding new possibilities within challenges. Imagine encountering a roadblock on your journey. You can see it as the end of the path—or you can view it as an opportunity to find a better way forward. The choice is yours, and that choice determines whether you feel stuck or empowered.

Here's a small shift that makes a big difference: Instead of seeing failure as a sign that something went wrong, try seeing it as part of the process. Every setback carries a lesson—something you can use to move forward smarter and stronger.

Embracing the Unknown as a Canvas for Growth

Most of us crave certainty. We want to know what's going to

happen next. But the truth is, the unknown isn't something to fear—it's a blank canvas, waiting for you to create something new. Transformation requires the courage to step into the unknown, trusting that the next step will reveal itself in time.

This isn't about being reckless; it's about being open. When you approach the unknown with curiosity rather than fear, you give yourself the freedom to grow. Each step into uncertainty becomes an adventure—an opportunity to discover new possibilities.

From Resistance to Flow
Many people resist change because it feels uncomfortable, but resistance only creates more struggle. Transformation happens when you move from resistance to flow—when you stop fighting against change and start moving with it. It's like swimming in a river. If you try to fight the current, you exhaust yourself. But if you learn to move with the flow, you find a sense of ease, even when the waters are rough.

Think of a writer so absorbed in crafting a story that hours slip by unnoticed, or a musician lost in the rhythm of a song. In those moments, the distinction between work and joy disappears—this is the essence of flow.

The key is to trust the process. Transformation doesn't always make sense in the moment, but with time, the pieces begin to fall into place. You'll look back and realize that every twist and turn was leading you somewhere meaningful.

Section 3: Shifting from Control to Trust

One of the greatest challenges in transformation is learning to release control. We're wired to seek certainty—we plan, strategize, and try to predict outcomes to feel safe. But the truth is, transformation rarely follows a straight path. It demands that we let go of the illusion of control and step into a space of trust.

Control says, *"I need to know how this ends before I begin."* Trust, on the other hand, whispers, *"I'll take the next step and let the path unfold."* This shift from control to trust is essential for growth because transformation isn't something you can force. It's something you allow.

"Growth is painful. Change is painful. But nothing is as painful as staying stuck somewhere you don't belong." — Alavida

The Courage to Surrender
Surrendering doesn't mean giving up—it means accepting what you can't change and focusing on what you can. It's the moment you stop resisting reality and start working with it. Think of it like planting a seed. You can't force it to grow, but you can water it, care for it, and trust that in time, it will sprout. The same is true for personal growth—it happens when you nurture the process and trust that things will come together, even if you can't see it yet.

Trusting Yourself Through Uncertainty
Letting go of control also means trusting yourself. It's believing that no matter what happens, you have the ability to navigate whatever comes your way. Trust isn't about knowing all the answers—it's about knowing that you'll figure things out as you

go. This self-trust builds resilience, giving you the confidence to embrace challenges with curiosity rather than fear.

The Magic of Unexpected Outcomes
Some of the most beautiful transformations happen when things don't go as planned. When you stop clinging to specific outcomes, you open yourself to possibilities you hadn't considered. It's like setting out to paint one picture, only to find that the brushstrokes take you somewhere unexpected—somewhere even better than you imagined.

This is the paradox of transformation: The more you try to control it, the more rigid and limited it becomes. But when you release control and embrace trust, you allow space for magic—those unexpected moments when life surprises you with something greater than you could have planned.

Section 4: The Story of the Lighthouse Keeper in the Storm

On the edge of a rocky cliff, overlooking the vast ocean, stood an old lighthouse. It had weathered many storms, guiding countless ships safely to shore. Inside the lighthouse lived a keeper—a quiet, resilient man who understood the sea's fury and the importance of his solitary duty. His only task was simple yet vital: to keep the light burning, no matter how fierce the storm.

One night, a violent storm rolled in. The winds howled, waves crashed against the rocks, and the sky was an unbroken curtain of darkness. Inside the lighthouse, the keeper felt the walls tremble as the storm raged. It would have been easy to give in to fear or exhaustion, to abandon his post and assume the ships could find their way. But he knew better.

He knew that even if no ships passed that night, his duty remained the same: to keep the light burning. As he climbed the steps, lantern in hand, a thought crossed his mind: 'Will anyone even notice if I stop?' But deep down, he knew the answer didn't matter—because the light was his responsibility, whether or not anyone saw it.
He climbed the winding stairs, his lantern in hand, and checked the flame. It flickered, fragile in the face of the storm, but it held. Hour by hour, he maintained the light, knowing that his small actions made all the difference.

At dawn, the storm subsided, revealing a battered but unbroken sea. A ship appeared on the horizon, its sails tattered but intact. As the keeper watched it pass, he felt no need for recognition— he had done what he was meant to do. His task was not about glory but about consistency, about showing up even when no one was watching.

The Lesson in the Lighthouse
This story reminds us that transformation is not always about grand, visible change. Sometimes, it's about holding steady in the storm, keeping the light burning even when everything around you feels dark. Just as the lighthouse keeper stayed committed to his purpose through the storm, we, too, must stay committed to our personal growth, especially when the path is difficult.

Transformation isn't always dramatic—it's often subtle, unfolding in small, consistent actions that build over time. The light we keep burning through difficult moments becomes a beacon, not only for ourselves but for others navigating their own storms. Even when it feels like no one notices, your actions matter.

Transformation comes from showing up, staying true to your purpose, and trusting that the light you carry makes a difference.

Section 5: Integrating Transformation into Daily Life

Transformation isn't something that happens all at once—it's a daily practice. It's in the small choices you make, the habits you build, and the mindset you carry with you. Each day offers an opportunity to grow, shift, and become more aligned with your purpose. The key to lasting transformation isn't just about achieving a goal; it's about integrating change into the way you live your life every day.

Transformation Through Micro-Changes
Big changes often start with small steps. It's not about waiting for the perfect moment or a grand breakthrough—it's about the little things you do consistently. Whether it's deciding to eat a healthier meal, taking five minutes to reflect, or choosing to respond with kindness in a tough moment, these micro-changes build momentum. Transformation unfolds one decision at a time.

Creating New Patterns Through Daily Practice
One of the most effective ways to sustain transformation is by creating new patterns through intentional habits. For example:

- **Morning rituals**: Set the tone for your day by grounding yourself with meditation, journaling, or physical movement.
- **Evening reflections**: Take a moment to assess your progress, reflect on what went well, and identify areas for growth.
- **Gratitude practice**: Cultivate a positive mindset by listing three things you're grateful for each day.

These practices reinforce the changes you're working toward, making transformation a natural part of your life.

The Power of Self-Compassion in Transformation
Transformation isn't linear—there will be setbacks, doubts, and moments when progress feels slow. In those moments, self-compassion becomes essential. Instead of judging yourself harshly, practice treating yourself with kindness. Recognize that growth takes time, and each step forward—no matter how small—is part of the journey.

Living the Process, Not Just the Outcome
Transformation is not just about reaching a destination; it's about who you become along the way. When you focus only on the outcome, you miss the beauty of the process. But when you learn to embrace the journey, every step becomes meaningful. The goal isn't just to change—it's to evolve into someone who can navigate life with purpose, resilience, and trust.

A friend once decided that each day, no matter how tired or busy, she would write down three things she was grateful for. At first, it felt trivial—but over time, this small habit became a lifeline, shifting her focus from stress to joy.

Carrying the Light Forward
Just like the lighthouse keeper who kept the flame alive through the storm, you carry your own light through the challenges of life. Transformation isn't about never facing storms—it's about learning to shine through them. Each time you integrate change into your daily life, you strengthen your light and become a beacon for others.

Chapter 7: Building Resilience

Section 1: Understanding Resilience – The Power of Mental Flexibility

**"The mind is like a parachute—it only works when it's open"
— Frank Zappa,**

Resilience isn't about sheer strength or willpower—it's about adaptability. Imagine a tree swaying in the wind. The ones that stand rigid, unwilling to move, are more likely to break. But the ones that bend, flex, and adjust with the wind's force survive the storm. This is the essence of resilience: the ability to adapt, adjust, and move forward, even when circumstances become difficult.

The Mindset Shift: Moving from Fixed to Flexible
At its core, resilience is rooted in mental flexibility—the capacity to shift your perspective when the unexpected happens. Many people fall into the trap of rigid thinking, believing there's only one path to success. But resilience is about recognizing that setbacks and detours aren't dead ends; they're invitations to explore new ways forward.

For example, instead of thinking, *"This plan didn't work; everything is ruined,"* try shifting the narrative: *"This is an opportunity to find another way."* It's not about denying challenges—it's about facing them with a mindset that says, *"There's always something I can do."*

Embracing Impermanence: The Nature of Change
Life is in constant motion. The seasons change, relationships evolve, and circumstances shift. Resilience is about learning to ride these waves of change without being swept away by them. It's not about avoiding discomfort—it's about building the capacity to face discomfort with courage. Every challenge becomes an opportunity to grow, to discover new strengths within yourself.

Resilience as a Skill You Build Over Time
The good news is that resilience isn't a trait you're either born with or without—it's a skill you develop through experience. Each challenge you encounter, whether big or small, is an opportunity to strengthen this skill. Think of it like building a muscle: the more you exercise it, the stronger it becomes.

Start with the small things. Maybe it's recovering quickly after receiving negative feedback at work or staying calm during a hectic day. Each time you navigate a setback and regain your balance, you add a layer to your resilience.

A Practical Exercise: Strengthening Your Resilience Muscle
Here's a simple practice to help you build resilience in everyday life:

1. **Pause and Reflect:** When something challenging happens, pause for a moment. Acknowledge the emotions you're feeling without judgment.
2. **Reframe the Situation:** Ask yourself, *What can I learn from this? How can this challenge serve my growth?*
3. **Choose Your Response:** Instead of reacting impulsively, take a deep breath and decide how you want to respond. This practice builds the habit of thoughtful action, even under pressure.

Resilience is not about perfection; it's about progress. Each time you recover from a setback, no matter how small, you strengthen your ability to navigate life's uncertainties. Over time, resilience becomes second nature—a steady presence that guides you through both calm and stormy seas.

Once we understand that resilience means bending with life's winds, the next step is learning how to rise from the ashes when life's storms knock us down.

Section 2: The Phoenix and the Ashes – Embracing Failure as Fuel for Growth

Failure has a way of making us question everything—our abilities, our choices, and even our worth. But failure isn't the end of the road; it's part of the process. Resilience is about learning to rise from the ashes, stronger and wiser than before. Just like the mythical phoenix, we each have the power to rebuild, no matter how devastating the fall.

The Story of the Phoenix and the Ashes
Once upon a time, there was an entrepreneur named Daniel who built his dream company from the ground up. For years, everything seemed to go right. Business boomed, profits soared, and Daniel believed he had it all figured out. But then, without warning, the market shifted, and his business began to crumble. Contracts were canceled, clients disappeared, and within a few months, Daniel found himself filing for bankruptcy.

In those first few weeks, Daniel felt like a ship without a compass, drifting between self-doubt and fear. But somewhere amidst the silence, he heard a whisper: 'This isn't the end—it's a lesson.'

It felt like the end of everything. His identity had been tied to his success, and without it, he felt lost. But as he sat among the wreckage of his dreams, something unexpected happened. He realized that failure wasn't a reflection of his worth—it was feedback. It was the universe's way of showing him what needed to change.

Daniel took time to reflect on what went wrong, not with bitterness, but with curiosity. He realized that his business had been built on trends, not long-term value. So, he began again, this time focusing on what mattered most—creating something meaningful, not just profitable. It wasn't easy, and there were moments when doubt crept in, but Daniel stayed the course. Slowly, step by step, he rebuilt his life.

Years later, his new business thrived, not because it was perfect, but because Daniel had grown through the process. Like the phoenix rising from the ashes, he discovered that failure wasn't the end—it was the beginning of something better.

The Power of Resilience in the Face of Failure
This story reminds us that resilience isn't about avoiding failure—it's about rising from it. Failure teaches us lessons that success never could. Each time you fall and get back up, you grow stronger. The key is to view failure not as a verdict but as a teacher.

Reframing Setbacks as Stepping Stones
When setbacks happen, it's easy to feel defeated. But resilience asks you to reframe the experience. Instead of asking, *"Why did this happen to me?"* ask, *"What can I learn from this?"* Every failure holds a lesson if you're willing to look for it. It's not about erasing mistakes—it's about transforming them into stepping stones for future success.

Trusting the Process of Growth
Just like the phoenix needs to burn before it can rise, sometimes we need to go through difficult moments to reach new heights. Resilience isn't about avoiding the fire—it's about trusting that you can rise from it, no matter how intense the flames. Each setback becomes fuel for your growth, shaping you into someone who can navigate life's challenges with grace.

Section 3: Emotional Endurance – Staying Strong When Life Gets Tough

Resilience isn't just about bouncing back—it's about building the emotional endurance to stay strong during life's toughest moments. Emotional endurance is the ability to sit with discomfort without running from it, knowing that challenges are part of the journey. It's about holding steady, even when things feel uncertain, and trusting that every tough moment is shaping you into someone stronger.

Navigating Emotional Uncertainty
One of the hardest parts of resilience is dealing with the unknown. We crave certainty, but life is full of moments that leave us questioning: *What happens next? Will this ever get easier?* Emotional endurance teaches us to sit with those questions without needing immediate answers. It's about learning to be okay with not knowing and staying steady through the process.

Instead of reacting to discomfort, emotional endurance asks us to respond with patience. Just like training for a marathon, it's not about sprinting through difficult emotions—it's about pacing yourself, knowing that each step forward builds strength.

Anchoring Yourself in Meaningful Habits
One of the best ways to build emotional endurance is by grounding yourself in simple, meaningful habits. These habits become your emotional anchors, keeping you steady through life's ups and downs. Here are a few examples:

- **Morning routines that center you:** A mindful practice like journaling, stretching, or a short meditation.
- **Evening check-ins:** Reflect on what went well during the day and release what didn't.
- **Gratitude journaling:** Write down three things you're grateful for, even on difficult days.

These small actions may seem insignificant, but over time, they build emotional strength, giving you a solid foundation to rely on during hard times.

Learning to Trust the Process
Emotional endurance is about trusting that the challenges you're facing have meaning, even if you can't see it yet. It's like climbing a mountain—you may not know how far you've come until you reach the top and look back. Trusting the process means knowing that every step forward counts, even when progress feels invisible.

Connection as a Source of Strength
Endurance isn't built in isolation. Sharing your struggles with people you trust provides relief and reminds you that you're not alone. Whether it's a friend, family member, or mentor, connection strengthens emotional resilience by reminding you that others are walking alongside you on this journey.

A marathon runner once said that the hardest part isn't the miles—it's the moments of doubt along the way. But by focusing on one step at a time, she found the strength to keep going.

Section 4: Redefining Success – Moving Beyond Setbacks

In our culture, success is often measured by outcomes—winning, achieving, reaching goals. But life is rarely that neat. Resilience teaches us that success isn't just about achieving a goal; it's about learning and growing along the way, even when things don't go as planned.

Letting Go of Perfection
One of the most difficult lessons in resilience is releasing the

need for perfection. Setbacks are part of life, and trying to avoid them only leads to frustration. True success comes from moving beyond the fear of failure and embracing each experience as part of your growth. When you redefine success as progress rather than perfection, every step forward—no matter how small—counts.

Each small step—whether it's sending an email you've been dreading or showing up to the gym after a tough day—is worth celebrating. These small wins are the breadcrumbs that lead you toward your bigger goals.

Learning to Celebrate the Process
Resilience isn't just about bouncing back—it's about finding joy in the process, even when the results aren't perfect. Think of it like hiking a mountain. The goal isn't just to reach the top—it's to appreciate the journey along the way. The conversations with friends, the unexpected views, and even the sore muscles are all part of the experience. When you learn to celebrate the process, you find success in every step.

Resilience as a New Definition of Success
The ability to rise after a setback is one of the greatest indicators of success. When you redefine success as resilience, failure becomes part of the journey rather than the end of it. It's not about how quickly you reach your goals, but about how you respond when things don't go as expected. Success, in this light, is not about avoiding challenges—it's about becoming someone who can thrive through them.

Section 5: A Legacy of Resilience – Carrying the Lessons Forward

Resilience isn't just about surviving difficult moments—it's about what you carry with you from those experiences. Every challenge you face shapes who you become, adding layers of strength, wisdom, and character. The true value of resilience is not just in bouncing back but in learning to live with purpose, even through life's uncertainties.

The Ripple Effect of Resilience

Your resilience doesn't just impact you—it creates a ripple effect, influencing the people around you. When you rise after a setback, you inspire others to do the same. It might be a colleague who watches you navigate challenges with grace, or a friend who sees you rebuild after failure. Your example teaches others that it's possible to thrive, not just survive, through life's difficulties.

Resilience as a Daily Practice

Living with resilience isn't just about overcoming big challenges—it's about the small, everyday choices that shape your life. It's in how you respond to stress, how you treat yourself when things don't go as planned, and how you continue to move forward, even when the path feels unclear. Each time you choose to keep going, you add another brick to the foundation of your inner strength.

Creating a Legacy of Growth

Resilience isn't something you achieve—it's something you pass on. The lessons you learn from setbacks become part of your legacy, shaping how you show up in the world and how you inspire others to do the same. Just like a tree that weathers the storm, your resilience leaves behind roots that others can draw strength from.

Whether you realize it or not, every time you rise from the ashes, you create a legacy of growth—a legacy that shows others that failure isn't the end and that every step forward matters. Your journey becomes a reminder that resilience isn't about being perfect—it's about being present, persistent, and open to what life has to offer.

Think of your resilience as a candle in a dark room. Each time you light it, others around you find the courage to light theirs. And before you know it, the room is filled with light, shining far beyond what you could have imagined.

Chapter 8: The Art of Decision Making

Section 1: Clarity in the Chaos – Navigating Uncertainty

The hardest decisions often come when the path ahead is unclear. It's easy to feel overwhelmed by possibilities, paralyzed by the fear of making the wrong choice. But decision-making isn't about eliminating uncertainty—it's about finding clarity within it. Clarity doesn't come from knowing every answer in advance; it comes from trusting that you'll find your way, one step at a time.

The Art of Slowing Down
When faced with uncertainty, the instinct is often to rush toward a decision, hoping to escape the discomfort of not knowing. But clarity emerges when we slow down. Taking a moment to breathe, reflect, and observe can reveal paths that aren't

immediately obvious. In moments of confusion, slowing down isn't a sign of weakness—it's a sign of wisdom.

Try this: Before rushing into a decision, pause and take three deep breaths. In the space created by those breaths, ask yourself: *What's the smallest step I can take right now?* Sometimes, clarity comes not from a grand solution but from a small, deliberate action.

Learning to Sit with Uncertainty
We're wired to seek certainty, but life rarely offers it. Learning to sit with uncertainty is one of the most valuable skills in decision-making. The discomfort of the unknown isn't something to escape—it's something to embrace. When you can resist the urge to make a rushed decision, you give yourself space to explore options and gather insights.

Clarity doesn't always arrive instantly—it unfolds over time, like a photograph slowly developing in the darkroom. The key is patience: allowing the image to come into focus, trusting that you'll see what you need to when the time is right.

Moving from Fear to Curiosity
Many people fear uncertainty because it feels like a loss of control. But what if the unknown wasn't a threat, but an invitation? What if every unknown held the potential for growth, discovery, or even a better outcome than you could have imagined? Curiosity opens the door to possibilities, replacing anxiety with wonder.

A sailor once found himself lost at sea, with no stars visible to guide him. Rather than panic, he adjusted his sails and headed toward the horizon, trusting that the stars would appear in time. And they did—only because he kept moving forward, step by step, even in the dark.

The truth is, no decision is ever perfect. But when you approach decision-making with curiosity rather than fear, you free yourself from the need for perfection. The goal isn't to make the perfect choice—it's to make the choice that aligns with your values, knowing that even if the path shifts, you'll find your way.

Section 2: The Power of Small Decisions – Building Momentum

We often think that big decisions define our lives, but it's the small, everyday choices that shape who we become. These seemingly insignificant decisions—what time you wake up, whether you follow through on a promise, or how you respond to a difficult moment—set the direction of your life. When small decisions align with your values and long-term vision, they create momentum that carries you forward, even when the bigger picture is unclear.

The Compound Effect of Small Choices

Every small decision acts like a brick in the foundation of your future. Skipping a workout or postponing a conversation might not seem like a big deal in the moment, but over time, these choices add up. Similarly, choosing to show up for yourself—whether it's by exercising for 10 minutes or reading a single page—builds momentum. Success isn't built overnight; it's the result of consistent, intentional choices.

"In any moment of decision, the best thing you can do is the right thing, the next best thing is the wrong thing, and the worst thing you can do is nothing." —Theodore Roosevelt

There's a famous story about an Olympic coach who told his athletes: "You don't need to be perfect every day. Just aim to be 1% better than yesterday." Those small, incremental improvements built over time led to gold medals—not because the athletes were extraordinary every day, but because they stayed consistent.

The Beauty of Simplicity

The beauty of small decisions is that they are manageable. You don't need to overhaul your life overnight to make progress. All you need to do is make the next right choice, however small it may seem. This simplicity takes the pressure off, shifting the focus from achieving perfection to staying on course. Even when life feels chaotic, small decisions ground you and remind you that you are still in control of your path.

Creating Systems that Support Your Decisions

The key to building momentum with small decisions is to create systems that make those choices easier. Systems take the guesswork out of decision-making, allowing good habits to become automatic. For example, if your goal is to write more, setting a 10-minute timer each day makes the decision to start easier. If you want to prioritize health, laying out your workout clothes the night before removes friction in the morning.

Small, thoughtful decisions compound over time, and sometimes a single, well-timed action has the power to change everything. Consider the story of a factory with a stalled conveyor belt...

The Right Screw at the Right Time

At a bustling factory that processed packages around the clock, a conveyor belt was the heart of the operation. The belt ran 24/7, and any breakdown would bring the entire factory to a halt, costing thousands in lost productivity every minute.

One day, the belt stopped suddenly. Panic set in as packages piled up, and no one could figure out what had gone wrong. After hours of failed attempts, the factory owner called in an expert technician with years of experience.

When the technician arrived, he didn't ask many questions. Instead, he went straight to the control panel, opened it, and inspected the wiring inside. After a few moments of silence, he pulled out a small screwdriver and carefully tightened a single screw. The conveyor belt whirred back to life instantly, and the factory was back in motion.

The factory owner was relieved but surprised. "That's all it took?" he asked. "One turn of a screw?"

The technician nodded and handed over his bill: $10,000.

The owner's jaw dropped. "Ten thousand dollars? But all you did was tighten a screw!"

The technician smiled. "Tightening the screw costs $1. Knowing which screw to tighten? That's $9,999."

Just like the expert knew which screw to tighten, building momentum in your life means focusing on small, intentional decisions that align with your goals. These seemingly insignificant actions pave the way for meaningful progress.

If you want to build a reading habit, placing a book on your nightstand ensures it's the first thing you see at bedtime. If your goal is to eat healthier, prepping meals on Sundays makes it easier to stay on track throughout the week.

Each small decision reinforces the story you tell yourself about who you are. Skipping a workout might seem insignificant, but over time, it shapes the belief that you're someone who gives up. Conversely, choosing to exercise—no matter how briefly—reinforces the identity of someone who values their health. These small systems build trust with yourself. Every time you follow through, you reinforce the belief that you are capable.

A Daily Practice for Momentum

At the end of each day, reflect on the small choices you made. Ask yourself: *"Did today's decisions align with the person I want to become?"* This practice helps you stay intentional, ensuring that each small step builds toward your long-term vision. And when things don't go perfectly, your systems help you get back on track without losing momentum. Progress isn't about perfection—it's about showing up, day after day, and trusting that each small step counts.

Section 3: Decision Fatigue and Overcoming Analysis Paralysis

We often imagine that indecision comes from laziness or a lack of willpower, but more often, it's the result of mental overload—the sheer number of decisions we face every day. Psychologists call this phenomenon decision fatigue: the more choices we make throughout the day, the harder it becomes to make thoughtful decisions. It's no wonder we often defer important decisions to "tomorrow" or avoid them entirely.

The Burden of Too Many Choices
In our fast-paced world, we're bombarded with options at every turn—what to eat, what to wear, how to spend our time, and even what to say in conversations. Each of these small decisions consumes mental energy, leaving us with less clarity for the bigger decisions that matter most. As mental energy declines, so does the quality of our decisions, leading to avoidance or impulsive choices. This is where procrastination sneaks in—not from a lack of motivation but from cognitive exhaustion.

Consider this: When you come home after a long day, you might find it difficult to choose between healthy food and fast food, not because you lack discipline, but because you've spent the entire day making decisions. The more energy spent on trivial decisions, the harder it becomes to focus on the ones that matter.

Overcoming Analysis Paralysis
Another form of procrastination comes from over-analyzing a decision—getting stuck in what's known as analysis paralysis. This happens when we believe that every choice must be perfect and free from risk, leading to endless research and second-guessing. Ironically, the longer we delay, the more overwhelming the decision becomes.

"Life can only be understood backwards; but it must be lived forwards." —Søren Kierkegaard

To break free from analysis paralysis, it's important to shift the focus from perfect outcomes to progress. Instead of trying to predict every possible outcome, ask yourself: *"What's the next best step I can take right now?"* This reframe shifts your energy from overthinking into action.

How Systems Reduce Decision Fatigue

One of the most effective ways to combat decision fatigue is by building systems and routines. Systems take the guesswork out of daily decisions, conserving your mental energy for what matters most. For example:

- Morning Routines: Having a structured morning—like setting out clothes the night before—reduces decision-making early in the day, leaving more energy for important tasks.
- Pre-Commitments: Deciding in advance to attend a workout class or block time for deep work removes the mental friction of choosing in the moment.
- Simplifying Choices: Successful individuals like Steve Jobs famously wore the same outfit every day to minimize trivial decisions, freeing up energy for strategic thinking.

The Power of Action Over Perfection

Procrastination often stems from the fear of making the wrong decision. But here's the truth: Decisions rarely need to be perfect—they just need to be made. Waiting for the perfect moment often leads to missed opportunities, while small actions create momentum, even if the outcome isn't certain.

A simple mantra to remember: *"Done is better than perfect."* The act of taking one small step today—whether sending an email, starting a draft, or making a phone call—builds momentum and signals to your brain that progress is possible. Over time, these small wins reduce the emotional weight of procrastination.

Simplify, Start, and Trust the Process
Breaking free from decision fatigue and analysis paralysis requires a combination of simplicity, action, and trust. Simplify your choices where you can, take one small step forward, and trust that the process will unfold as you go. Not every decision will be perfect, but each one will move you closer to clarity and momentum.

Procrastination is not a reflection of your abilities—it's a signal that something needs to change. The good news? The moment you decide to take one step forward, however small, you begin to shift the energy in your favor. And each time you act, you prove to yourself that you are capable of moving through uncertainty with confidence.

Section 4: Confidence in Decision-Making – Trusting Your Path

The hardest part of decision-making is often trusting the path you choose. Doubt creeps in, making you wonder if you've made the right choice. But clarity doesn't always arrive before a decision—it often unfolds as you walk the path you've chosen. Confidence in decision-making isn't about knowing every answer in advance; it's about trusting yourself to figure things out along the way.

The Story of the Wise Woman at the Crossroads

One day, a traveler reached a fork in the road. Exhausted and confused, he sat down at the crossroads, unsure which path to take. As he sat, a wise woman appeared, carrying a small lantern that flickered gently in the dusk.

The traveler asked her, "Which road should I take? How will I know which one is right?"

The wise woman smiled and said, "Every choice creates two realities—the one you choose and the one you leave behind. It's not the road that defines you, but the way you walk the path you choose."

Still uncertain, the traveler asked, "But what if I choose the wrong path?"

The woman knelt beside him and whispered, "There is no perfect path. But each step you take creates the clarity you seek. If you hesitate too long, you'll miss the beauty waiting down either road. The only mistake is not moving at all."

With a nod of understanding, the traveler rose and took his first step down one of the roads. As he walked, he felt the weight of indecision lift. The journey wasn't perfect, but with each step, the path grew clearer. And soon, he realized that the journey itself was the reward, not the destination.

The Power of Committing to Your Decisions

Just like the traveler at the crossroads, the key to confident decision-making is to commit fully to the path you choose. Indecision drains energy, but commitment builds momentum.

When you trust yourself to make a choice—and stick with it—you remove the weight of hesitation.

The truth is, you don't need to know every answer right now. Sometimes, the act of deciding is what brings clarity. As the wise woman said, "Each step creates the clarity you seek."

How to Strengthen Decision-Making Confidence
Confidence grows through practice. The more you make decisions—big or small—the more you reinforce your trust in your ability to handle uncertainty. Here are a few ways to strengthen your decision-making muscles:

1. Set Deadlines for Decisions:

    Giving yourself a timeline prevents overthinking. Decisions made within a reasonable window are more likely to align with your intuition.
2. Use the Two-Minute Rule:

    If a decision will take less than two minutes to make—like sending a quick email or replying to a text—do it immediately. This reduces mental clutter and creates space for bigger decisions.
3. Make Small Commitments Daily:

    Each small decision reinforces the habit of commitment. Whether it's choosing to read a chapter of a book or going for a walk, every follow-through strengthens your decision-making confidence.

Releasing the Fear of Mistakes

One of the biggest barriers to confident decision-making is the fear of making mistakes. But mistakes aren't signs of failure—they're opportunities for growth. Each misstep teaches you something valuable about yourself and the world around you. The real mistake is not in choosing the wrong path but in failing to act at all.

As the traveler learned at the crossroads, no decision is wasted. Every choice shapes your journey, offering lessons that guide you forward. The key is to release the need for perfection and embrace the process of growth.

Trust the Path, Trust Yourself
In the end, decision-making isn't about having all the answers—it's about having the courage to act, knowing that clarity will come along the way. Each step you take, no matter how uncertain, builds confidence. And with confidence, you create momentum that carries you toward your vision, even when the path ahead is unclear.

Section 5: Aligned Decisions – Creating Freedom and Fulfillment

Decision-making isn't just about picking the right option—it's about creating a life that aligns with your values. When your daily choices reflect what matters most to you, they form a foundation of inner freedom—freedom from doubt, hesitation, and regret. This alignment makes even small decisions feel meaningful, building toward a future you can be proud of.

Freedom Through Aligned Choices

True freedom doesn't come from eliminating uncertainty; it comes from trusting yourself to navigate uncertainty with clarity and purpose. When your decisions align with your values, there's no need for second-guessing. Each choice becomes a step forward, whether it's easy or difficult, because it reflects who you are and what you stand for.

Think of someone who decides to live a healthier lifestyle. The small choice to drink water instead of soda might seem trivial, but it reflects a deeper commitment to well-being. Over time, these small, intentional decisions create a life that feels in alignment with that person's health goals. This is the essence of freedom—not the absence of choices, but the confidence that each choice aligns with your values.

How Aligned Decisions Build Fulfillment
We often think of fulfillment as something we achieve after accomplishing big goals, but the truth is, fulfillment is built step by step, through the decisions we make every day. When your actions align with your long-term vision, every small choice becomes meaningful. Fulfillment isn't found in the final destination; it's created in the way you walk your path.

- Saying yes to meaningful opportunities and no to distractions builds a sense of purpose.
- Taking small steps toward your dreams each day creates momentum, even when progress feels slow.
- Acting in alignment with your values, even in difficult moments, builds self-trust and inner peace.

Aligned decision-making transforms your life into a series of intentional steps, each one reinforcing the person you are becoming.

The Courage to Say No
One of the most powerful aspects of aligned decision-making is the ability to say no—not out of fear, but out of clarity. Saying no to what doesn't serve you creates space for what does. It's a reminder that not every opportunity aligns with your purpose, and that's okay. When you make decisions from a place of clarity, every no becomes a gift to yourself—a commitment to stay on course.

A helpful mantra:
"Every no is a yes to something better."

Each time you say no to distractions, unnecessary obligations, or fear-based choices, you create room for the things that matter most. This clarity brings freedom, knowing that your decisions are moving you in the direction you truly want to go.

A Daily Practice for Aligned Decision-Making
Building the habit of aligned decision-making doesn't require perfection—it requires awareness and intentionality. Here's a simple practice to help you stay aligned:

1. Morning Intention: At the start of each day, ask yourself: *What is one decision I can make today that aligns with my values?*
2. Midday Check-In: Pause halfway through your day to reflect: *Am I staying on course? If not, what small adjustment can I make?*
3. Evening Reflection: Before bed, ask yourself: *Did today's decisions align with the person I want to become?*

This practice helps you stay connected to your values, creating momentum and fulfillment through small, intentional decisions.

Building a Life You Can Trust

"**As you start to walk on the way, the way appears.**" — Rumi
In the end, aligned decision-making is about more than just making good choices—it's about building a life you can trust. Each time you make a decision that reflects your values, you strengthen your relationship with yourself. This trust creates freedom, knowing that no matter what life throws your way, you'll navigate it with clarity, confidence, and purpose.

Aligned decision-making isn't about perfection—it's about showing up every day, making choices that matter, and trusting the journey as it unfolds. With each aligned decision, you build a life that feels meaningful—not because it's free of uncertainty, but because it's filled with intentionality and purpose.

Chapter 9: Nurturing Creativity and Innovation

Section 1: Embracing Creativity – Everyone's Creative Potential

"The creation of something new is not accomplished by the intellect but by the play instinct acting from inner necessity."
—Carl Jung

Many people believe that creativity is a gift reserved for a select few—artists, musicians, or inventors. But the truth is, creativity lives within all of us. It's not about being the most talented painter or coming up with world-changing inventions; it's about thinking in new ways, solving problems creatively, and approaching life with curiosity.

Creativity isn't something you either have or don't—it's a muscle that grows with practice. Every time you experiment with a new recipe, brainstorm solutions at work, or find a way to entertain your kids on a rainy day, you're exercising your creative mind. Creativity isn't about perfection—it's about exploration and openness to new experiences.

Breaking Through the Myth of Talent
One of the biggest barriers to creativity is the belief that only talented people can be creative. But as researchers have shown, creativity is not innate—it's developed through practice and effort. Famous innovators like Thomas Edison didn't succeed because they were born geniuses—they succeeded because they failed over and over until they found solutions. Edison's famous quote captures it well: *"I have not failed. I've just found 10,000 ways that won't work."*

The same principle applies to everyday life: Creativity grows when you give yourself permission to try, fail, and learn. When you stop worrying about being perfect, you create space for ideas to flow.

Curiosity as the Fuel for Creativity
At the heart of creativity is curiosity—the desire to explore, ask questions, and see the world from new perspectives. Curiosity invites us to look beyond the surface and discover connections we might not have noticed before. The more curious you are, the more creative you become.

Here's a simple way to practice: Every day, challenge yourself to ask one new question—about your work, your relationships, or even the world around you. Questions like *"What if we tried it this way?"* or *"How else could this problem be solved?"* spark creative thinking and encourage innovation.

The Role of Play in Unlocking Creativity
Creativity thrives in environments that encourage playfulness. When we're too focused on getting things right, we block the flow of ideas. Play allows us to experiment without fear of failure. Think about children—when they draw or build, they're not worried about whether their creation is "good." They're fully immersed in the joy of creating.

As adults, we often lose that sense of play because we become too focused on outcomes. But reclaiming a playful mindset can unlock your creative potential. Here's a practice: Set aside 10 minutes each day for playful experimentation—try doodling, writing nonsense poetry, or building something with no goal in mind. You'll be surprised at how quickly your mind begins to generate new ideas when you let go of expectations.

Creativity as a Way of Life
Creativity isn't just something you do—it's a way of being open to the world. It's about approaching challenges with a mindset that says, *"What if?"* and viewing obstacles as opportunities for growth. When you nurture creativity in your daily life, it becomes a lens through which you see the world—a tool that helps you solve problems, connect with others, and grow as a person.

Everyone Is Creative
Creativity isn't reserved for a select few—it's within all of us. The key is to give yourself permission to explore, play, and stay curious. When you embrace creativity as a way of life, you'll find

new solutions to challenges, build deeper connections with others, and unlock potential you didn't know you had.

Section 2: Creating Space for Innovation – The Power of Stillness and Reflection

In a world that's always moving, innovation requires us to slow down. It's easy to think that creativity and innovation thrive in constant motion, but some of the most groundbreaking ideas emerge from moments of stillness. When we step back from the noise, we give our minds space to reflect, connect ideas, and spark innovation.

"All of humanity's problems stem from man's inability to sit quietly in a room alone." — Blaise Pascal

Innovation Needs Space to Breathe
When we're constantly busy—checking emails, rushing through tasks, or filling every moment with activity—our minds don't have the chance to wander. But mental stillness is essential for innovation. It's in those quiet moments—while walking, journaling, or simply daydreaming—that ideas often click into place.

Consider Albert Einstein, who said that some of his best ideas came to him while playing the violin. Stepping away from focused work and allowing the mind to relax opens the door to unexpected insights.

Here's a practice: Schedule unstructured time each day. Take a walk without your phone or spend a few minutes journaling your thoughts without a specific goal. These moments of stillness invite new ideas to emerge naturally.

The Role of Reflection in Innovation

Reflection is where ideas go to take root. Just like seeds need time in the soil to grow, ideas need time to develop through thoughtful reflection. Reflection allows you to connect the dots between experiences, uncover patterns, and see opportunities you might have missed.

Try this: At the end of each day, ask yourself three reflection questions:

1. What sparked my curiosity today?
2. Did I encounter any challenges, and what did I learn from them?
3. Is there an idea I've been sitting on that deserves attention?

These small moments of reflection cultivate self-awareness and help you identify areas ripe for innovation.

Silence and Solitude as Tools for Innovation

Innovation isn't always born in brainstorming meetings or group discussions—it often thrives in silence and solitude. Many great thinkers throughout history—from Virginia Woolf to Steve Jobs—recognized the value of stepping away from the crowd to cultivate their best ideas.

Solitude isn't about isolation—it's about creating intentional space for deep thinking. When you're alone with your thoughts, you can explore ideas without distraction.

If sitting in silence feels uncomfortable, start small: Spend five minutes each day unplugged and alone. Let your thoughts wander without judgment. Over time, you'll find that these moments of solitude become fertile ground for creativity.

Balancing Action with Reflection
While stillness is essential, innovation also requires action. The key is to find a balance between reflection and movement—a rhythm that allows you to generate ideas and bring them to life. Think of it like breathing: Inhale with reflection, exhale with action. Both are necessary for creativity to flow.

Reflection fuels innovation by giving you clarity, and action brings those ideas to life. The combination of both ensures that creativity doesn't stay locked in your mind but transforms into real-world solutions.

Innovation Thrives in Stillness
The modern world often pushes us to keep moving, but innovation requires moments of stillness and reflection. By slowing down and creating space for your thoughts, you invite fresh ideas to surface. Balance reflection with action, and you'll discover that innovation isn't something you have to force—it's something you can nurture.

Section 3: Overcoming Creative Blocks – Finding Flow

Every creative journey hits roadblocks—those frustrating moments when ideas won't flow, and inspiration feels far away. But creative blocks aren't dead ends—they're signals. They often indicate that something within us needs to shift. Learning how to move through these blocks with patience and curiosity is essential to nurturing creativity.

Why Blocks Happen
Creative blocks can arise for many reasons—fear of failure, perfectionism, overwork, or lack of clarity. Sometimes, the pressure to be brilliant can choke creativity before it even begins. At other times, blocks emerge from mental fatigue or a need to recharge.

The key to overcoming these blocks isn't to fight them—it's to understand what they're telling you. Often, a block is a message: *Slow down. Shift perspectives. Try a new approach.*

The Practice of Letting Go
One of the most powerful ways to break through a creative block is to let go of expectations. When you stop demanding perfection, you make space for ideas to flow freely. A helpful practice is to create without a goal. Whether it's writing nonsense, doodling aimlessly, or brainstorming wild ideas—these playful moments often spark unexpected breakthroughs.

Cultivating Flow through Movement
Sometimes, the best way to unlock creativity is to step away from the task at hand. Movement—whether through walking, stretching, or dancing—engages the body and loosens mental knots. Many writers and artists report having their best ideas while walking, precisely because movement frees the mind.

Next time you feel stuck, try this: Get up, move around, and let your mind wander. You may find that the solution appears when you least expect it.

The Power of Constraints in Creativity

It may seem counterintuitive, but constraints often fuel creativity. When you have endless options, it's easy to get overwhelmed. But setting boundaries—like limiting yourself to a few materials or a specific time frame—forces you to be resourceful and inventive.

Consider this: Dr. Seuss wrote *Green Eggs and Ham* using only 50 words because of a bet. That constraint pushed his creativity, leading to one of the most beloved children's books of all time.

Finding Flow: Where Creativity Feels Effortless

Flow is that magical state where ideas pour out effortlessly, and time seems to dissolve. It's not something you can force—it happens when your skills match the challenge and you become fully absorbed in the process. Flow often emerges when you:

- Minimize distractions.
- Work in short, focused bursts.
- Engage in activities that challenge you but aren't overwhelming.

Once you find flow, you tap into creativity's most powerful force—the joy of creation for its own sake.

Creativity Thrives in the Freedom to Play and the Discipline to Persist

Creative blocks are part of the process, but they aren't roadblocks—they're invitations to try something new. When you let go of expectations, embrace movement, and set playful constraints, you create the conditions for flow to emerge. Remember: Creativity isn't always easy, but it's always worth the effort.

Section 4: The Story of The Alchemist's Apprentice

In a small village nestled between rolling hills, lived an old alchemist known for his remarkable ability to transform the simplest materials into valuable treasures. People traveled from far and wide, hoping to learn the secret of alchemy. One day, a young apprentice named Leo arrived, eager to uncover the mystery of turning lead into gold.

The alchemist welcomed Leo with a smile. "Alchemy is not about magic," the old man said. "It's about learning to see potential where others see nothing—and working patiently until the transformation unfolds."

The Apprentice's First Lesson: Play Before Perfection
Eager to begin, Leo asked for instructions. But instead of giving him a formula, the alchemist handed him a set of strange, mismatched tools. "Your task," the alchemist said, "is to experiment. Play with these materials, make mistakes, and come back to me in a week."

Frustrated, Leo protested. "But what if I do it wrong?"

The alchemist chuckled. "There is no wrong—only learning."

For the next few days, Leo tinkered endlessly. His experiments felt chaotic, and more often than not, they ended in failure. Yet, each time something didn't work, Leo found himself growing more curious. Slowly, he discovered that even mistakes carried hidden lessons.

The Second Lesson: Embrace the Unknown
After a week, Leo returned, disheartened by his messy attempts.

The alchemist smiled and said, "You're closer than you think. Alchemy requires trusting the unknown. Just as lead doesn't turn into gold in an instant, creativity unfolds in its own time."

Leo's next task was to create without worrying about the outcome. It was in these moments—when Leo stopped forcing results—that unexpected ideas began to emerge. He found beauty in unexpected combinations and solutions he hadn't anticipated.

The Final Lesson: Persistence and Patience
Weeks turned into months, and still, Leo hadn't produced gold. Frustration gnawed at him, but the alchemist remained patient. "Alchemy isn't just about results," the old man reminded him. "It's about falling in love with the process—trusting that each small step matters, even when progress is invisible."

Finally, one day, something clicked. Leo didn't just learn how to transform materials—he learned how to transform himself. The alchemy wasn't in turning lead into gold—it was in his newfound ability to see potential, persevere through failure, and create something valuable from the ordinary.

The Lesson of The Alchemist's Apprentice
Leo's journey is a reminder that creativity isn't about magic or luck—it's about patience, persistence, and a willingness to experiment. The greatest innovations come not from perfection, but from playing, trusting the unknown, and staying curious through the process.

Just like the apprentice, we are all alchemists in our own lives. Each time we turn an idea into action, we engage in a small act of alchemy—transforming thoughts into reality. And each time we persist through setbacks, we unlock the creative potential that lies within us.

The Process is the Alchemy

Creativity and innovation aren't about immediate results—they're about trusting the process and knowing that every experiment, every mistake, and every small step contributes to the final transformation. When we learn to love the process, we discover that the true alchemy lies not just in what we create—but in who we become along the way.

Section 5: Bringing Creativity to Life – Turning Ideas into Reality

Creativity isn't just about having ideas—it's about bringing them to life. The journey from concept to creation is where the magic happens, but it's also where most people get stuck. It's easy to dream up ideas, but turning them into reality requires effort, persistence, and courage. The real power of creativity lies not just in thinking differently, but in acting on your ideas and following through, even when the process feels messy or uncertain.

Creativity as a Practice, Not a Destination

Many people think of creativity as a destination—a moment when the perfect idea arrives fully formed. But creativity is a practice. It's about showing up every day, working on your craft, and embracing the messy middle. There will be false starts, failed experiments, and moments of doubt. But each step forward builds momentum, even if you can't see the full picture yet.

The key is to fall in love with the process of creating, not just the final result. Whether you're writing a book, starting a business, or solving a personal challenge, the creative journey will take you through ups and downs. But every effort—no matter how small—brings you closer to your goal.

The Courage to Act on Your Ideas
It's one thing to have an idea; it's another to take action. Many people get stuck in fear—fear of failure, rejection, or not being good enough. But creativity requires courage—the willingness to put your ideas out into the world, even when the outcome is uncertain.

Here's the truth: There will never be a perfect moment to start. The best way to bring creativity to life is to start where you are, with what you have. Every action—no matter how small—creates momentum, turning thoughts into reality. And with each step forward, your confidence grows.

Building a Creative Life Through Small Steps
Bringing creativity to life doesn't mean making grand gestures. It's the small, consistent steps that lead to transformation. Think of creativity as a garden—you need to plant seeds, water them regularly, and give them time to grow. Small actions, done consistently, nurture the creative spark within you and turn ideas into meaningful outcomes.

- Write one sentence a day if you want to finish a book.
- Brainstorm for five minutes daily if you're working on a new project.
- Experiment with small prototypes before launching something big.

These small actions create a ripple effect, building the foundation for larger breakthroughs over time.

Creativity as a Life Skill

Creativity isn't just for artists—it's a life skill that helps you solve problems, adapt to change, and thrive in uncertainty. Whether you're navigating a career shift, strengthening relationships, or pursuing personal growth, the ability to think creatively opens new possibilities.

When you make creativity part of your daily life, you develop the skills to innovate, solve challenges, and grow in ways you never imagined. Creativity becomes more than just a tool—it becomes a mindset that empowers you to create the life you want.

The Power of Action and Persistence

The difference between dreaming and creating lies in action and persistence. The journey of creativity isn't about waiting for inspiration—it's about starting, showing up, and following through, even when the path isn't clear. Creativity comes to life when you turn your ideas into actions, one small step at a time.

Chapter 10: Leadership and Influence

Section 1: The Essence of Leadership – Leading from Within

"Before you are a leader, success is all about growing yourself. When you become a leader, success is all about growing others." —Jack Welch

At its core, leadership is not about control—it's about influence. True leaders inspire people not by giving orders but by living their values and leading by example. Whether you're leading a team at work, guiding a family, or motivating a friend, leadership begins with who you are, not just what you do.

Influence Over Authority
Many people associate leadership with authority, but influence is more powerful than command. Influence isn't tied to a title or position—it's earned through trust, consistency, and authenticity.

The people who influence us the most aren't necessarily the ones in charge—they're the ones who inspire us to become better versions of ourselves.

Think of someone in your life who's had a positive impact—maybe a teacher, friend, or mentor. They probably didn't lead by demanding obedience but by inspiring trust and belief in your potential. That's the essence of leadership: helping others grow by embodying the qualities you want to inspire.

Leadership Begins with Self-Leadership
Before you can lead others, you must first learn to lead yourself. Self-leadership is the practice of taking responsibility for your own growth, actions, and mindset. It's about aligning your choices with your values and goals, even when no one is watching.

The best leaders are those who are continually working on themselves—improving their habits, expanding their knowledge, and staying grounded in their purpose. This personal alignment creates a foundation for authentic influence, making it easier to inspire and guide others.

The Power of Empathy in Leadership
Leadership isn't about having all the answers—it's about listening deeply and understanding the needs of those you lead. When leaders practice empathy, they create a space where people feel valued and understood. This emotional connection builds trust and loyalty, the cornerstones of influence.

Empathy also allows leaders to see challenges from different perspectives, helping them make better decisions. When you lead with empathy, you don't just direct people—you empower them to find their own solutions and grow through the process.

Leading by Example: Aligning Actions with Values
True leaders know that actions speak louder than words. People follow leaders they trust, and trust is built when words align with actions. It's easy to give advice or set expectations for others, but the real impact comes when you embody those principles yourself.

For example, if you want to foster a culture of honesty, start by being transparent in your own actions. If you value teamwork, model collaboration by being open to feedback and ideas from others. This alignment between values and behavior inspires others to follow your lead.

Leadership is a Daily Practice
Leadership isn't a one-time act—it's a daily practice. It starts with self-leadership, builds through empathy and example, and culminates in inspiring others to grow. Whether you're leading a team or guiding a friend, the essence of leadership lies not in controlling others but in empowering them to step into their own potential.

Section 2: The Power of Servant Leadership – Empowering Others to Thrive

When people think of leadership, they often picture someone at the top of a hierarchy, giving orders. But servant leadership flips that idea on its head. It's not about leading from above—it's about lifting others up. The most influential leaders aren't the ones focused on power; they're the ones committed to helping others succeed.

Leading by Serving

Servant leadership means putting the needs of others first. It's about supporting your team, guiding them through challenges, and helping them grow into their potential. This approach builds trust, loyalty, and a sense of community—qualities that traditional authority struggles to achieve.

Think of leaders like Mahatma Gandhi or Mother Teresa. Their influence didn't come from titles or positions—it came from their unwavering commitment to serving others. They showed the world that true leadership is about giving, not taking.

Creating Space for Others to Shine

One of the most powerful things a servant leader can do is create space for others to thrive. Instead of taking credit for success, they share it. Instead of dictating solutions, they empower others to find their own answers. This creates a culture where people feel valued and motivated to bring their best selves forward.

When you empower others, you multiply your influence. A great leader's legacy isn't just in what they accomplish—it's in the people they inspire to grow and succeed.

Humility as a Leadership Strength

At the heart of servant leadership is humility—the ability to recognize that leadership is about service, not status. Humility allows leaders to stay open to feedback, admit mistakes, and remain grounded in their values.

Humility also fosters deeper connections. When leaders show vulnerability and authenticity, they encourage those around them to do the same. This creates an environment where collaboration thrives and trust grows.

Leadership is About Empowering Others
Servant leadership is a reminder that true influence comes from service. When you lead by lifting others up, you create an environment where people feel empowered to succeed. Leadership isn't about being in charge—it's about helping others rise.

Section 3: Building Influence Through Trust and Consistency

Influence isn't about commanding others—it's about earning their trust over time. At its core, leadership is a relationship, and like all relationships, it thrives on trust and consistency. People follow leaders because they trust their character and believe in their reliability—not because of authority alone.

When you show up consistently, aligned with your values, trust naturally grows. Every small action becomes a building block for influence, creating a foundation others can rely on.

The Long Game of Trust
Trust is earned over time. It's built in small moments—when you follow through on promises, admit mistakes, and demonstrate empathy in difficult situations. Brené Brown says it best: ***"Trust is earned in the smallest moments."***

Consider a leader who consistently listens to their team, even when things are hectic. This leader builds trust because people know their concerns will be heard, no matter the situation. On the other hand, when words and actions don't align—like making promises but not following through—trust erodes, and influence weakens.

Trust isn't just a feel-good concept; it's the foundation for effective leadership. When people trust you, they feel safe—safe enough to take risks, share ideas, and grow. Without trust, innovation stalls, and relationships break down.

Practical Ways to Build Trust
Building trust requires more than good intentions—it's about consistent actions. Here are practical ways to cultivate trust in leadership:

- Active Listening: Pay attention when others speak and resist the urge to jump in with solutions too quickly. Listening shows respect and builds connection.
- Transparency: Be open about challenges and setbacks. When people see that you're honest, even when it's uncomfortable, trust grows.
- Reliability: Follow through on your commitments, no matter how small. Reliability builds confidence in your leadership over time.
- Admitting Mistakes: Vulnerability fosters trust. When leaders own up to their mistakes, it creates a culture where people feel safe to do the same.

Consistency: The Secret to Influence

Influence isn't built in grand gestures—it's the result of small, consistent actions that align with your values. Leadership requires showing up not only on good days but also when things get tough. Think about a parent or mentor who, through consistent support and guidance, becomes a lifelong influence. Their reliability provides a sense of stability and trust.

Consistency also means staying grounded in your values, even when circumstances change. When people know what to expect from you—when your actions consistently reflect your principles—they feel secure following your lead.

John Maxwell said it well:
"Leadership is not about titles, positions, or flowcharts. It is about one life influencing another."

Consistency allows that influence to grow naturally, one interaction at a time.

The Role of Vulnerability in Leadership
Many people think leadership means projecting strength at all times. But true leadership requires vulnerability—the willingness to admit that you don't have all the answers. Vulnerability isn't a weakness; it's a sign of authenticity and courage. It shows that you are human, just like those you lead.

When leaders demonstrate vulnerability—by asking for help, acknowledging uncertainties, or admitting mistakes—they invite others to do the same. This creates a culture of openness and trust, where people feel empowered to contribute and grow without fear of judgment.

Influence Grows Through Trust, Consistency, and Vulnerability

Building influence isn't about titles or authority—it's about earning trust through consistent, reliable actions. It's about showing up for others, staying aligned with your values, and leading by example. When leaders act with integrity and vulnerability, they create a space where people feel safe, respected, and motivated to thrive. Influence grows not through grand gestures but through small, consistent acts of trust.

Section 4: The Shepherd Who Became a Leader

In a quiet, rural village, nestled among rolling hills, lived a humble shepherd named Elias. Elias was not a man of power or influence—he spent his days tending to his small flock, guiding the sheep across vast meadows, ensuring they were safe from storms and predators. He was quiet, patient, and reliable, content with the simple rhythms of life.

One day, the village faced a crisis. A severe drought had dried up the river that supplied the town with water, and people began to panic. With no appointed leader to organize a plan, tempers flared, and chaos erupted. But amidst the confusion, Elias continued his quiet, steady work.

A Moment of Trust

One morning, as villagers debated what to do, someone noticed Elias preparing his flock to move. "Where are you going?" a young boy asked.

Elias smiled softly. "There's a hidden spring beyond the hills. If we move now, we can reach it before the sun becomes too hot."

The boy's mother overheard and turned to Elias. "Can we come with you? We have no idea where to find water."

Elias nodded. "You're welcome to join me, but it won't be easy. The path is steep, and the journey long."

Word spread, and soon a small group of villagers decided to follow the shepherd. Without fuss or fanfare, Elias led them through rugged terrain, using the same steady approach he had learned tending to his sheep—one step at a time, never rushing, always adjusting to the needs of the weakest in the group.

Leadership Through Service
Elias's approach was simple: lead from behind, ensure no one was left behind, and guide the group without imposing his will. When someone grew tired, he stopped to rest with them. When others felt afraid, he shared words of quiet encouragement. He did not see himself as their leader—he was simply serving as he always had.

Over time, the villagers began to trust him, not because he gave orders but because of his consistency and care. His actions spoke louder than words. Elias showed up every day, reliable and steady, ensuring both the sheep and villagers arrived safely, step by step.

A Journey of Growth
When they finally reached the hidden spring, the villagers rejoiced, filling their jars with fresh water. Someone turned to Elias and said, "You should have led us from the beginning. You're the kind of leader we need."

Elias shook his head with a smile. "I didn't lead you—I just walked with you."

The villagers were struck by his words. In that moment, they realized that true leadership isn't about power or authority—it's about service, humility, and trust. They had followed Elias not because he demanded it, but because he inspired it through his actions.

The Lesson of the Shepherd
Elias returned to his flock, but the villagers never forgot the lessons he had taught them. His quiet leadership became the model for how they approached challenges in the future: with patience, consistency, and care for one another.

The story of The Shepherd Who Became a Leader is a reminder that true leadership isn't about controlling others—it's about empowering them to succeed. Servant leaders don't seek the spotlight—they lead through actions, trust, and humility, inspiring others to grow and thrive.

Leadership is a Journey of Service
The story of Elias shows us that leadership isn't about titles or status—it's about how you show up for others. When leaders serve with humility, trust, and consistency, they build influence that lasts far beyond any crisis. Leadership is not about taking control—it's about walking alongside others and empowering them to grow.

Section 5: Leadership as a Legacy – Inspiring Future Generations

True leadership leaves a lasting impact, not through control or recognition but through the legacy it creates. Legacy isn't about personal glory—it's about the lives you touch and the people you empower along the way. When you inspire others to grow, they carry your influence forward, passing it on to future generations.

The Ripple Effect of Leadership

Every action you take as a leader creates a ripple effect, influencing those around you. Think of a teacher who inspires students, not just for the semester, but for years to come. Or a mentor who offers guidance during a tough moment, helping someone make a life-changing decision. These small acts of leadership extend far beyond the moment.

Leadership is not about what you achieve during your lifetime— it's about who you help others become. A good leader measures success not by personal accomplishments but by the growth of those they serve.

Empowering Others to Lead

The best leaders don't seek followers—they create more leaders. They pass on the tools, knowledge, and encouragement others need to grow into leadership roles. This creates a culture of empowerment, where each person feels confident taking initiative and contributing their unique strengths.

Legacy is built when leaders step back and allow others to shine. It's not about being indispensable but about making sure others have the skills and confidence to carry on the mission.

Leadership Beyond the Moment

One of the greatest challenges in leadership is knowing when to let go. Leadership is not about clinging to power or influence— it's about recognizing the right moment to pass the torch. Great leaders understand that their role is temporary, but the values and lessons they instill can last a lifetime.

"A leader is best when people barely know he exists, when his work is done, his aim fulfilled, they will say: we did it ourselves." —Lao Tzu

This quote reminds us that the greatest legacy a leader can leave is a community or team that thrives independently. When people feel empowered to lead themselves, the influence of their leader continues to ripple outward.

Leadership is a Legacy of Growth and Empowerment
Leadership isn't measured by titles or achievements—it's measured by the growth of those you serve. Every act of service, every word of encouragement, and every moment of trust contributes to a legacy that outlasts the leader.When leaders empower others to lead, they create a ripple effect that carries on through future generations.

Chapter 11: Achieving Work-Life Balance

Section 1: Balancing Priorities – Knowing What to Hold and What to Let Go

Imagine life as a juggling act. In one hand, you're holding rubber balls—the daily tasks, small obligations, and minor inconveniences. These balls, though important, will bounce back if dropped. On the other hand, you hold glass balls—the people, relationships, health, and moments that truly matter. If you drop these, the consequences are lasting.

The challenge is that many of us juggle life without understanding the difference between the rubber and glass balls. We treat everything with the same urgency, leading to stress, burnout, and frustration. True work-life balance comes when you know which balls to let fall and which ones must be carefully kept in hand.

I once knew a manager who was constantly focused on every small detail at work, treating every task as equally urgent. Over time, he found himself missing family events and sacrificing his health, all in the name of getting everything done. It wasn't until his health took a hit that he realized he had been juggling too many rubber balls and letting the glass ones—his health and relationships—fall. That wake-up call helped him refocus, ensuring the important things never slipped again.

The Illusion of Perfect Balance
It's easy to believe that work-life balance means giving equal time to everything, but that's unrealistic. Balance isn't about dividing your time evenly—it's about being fully present wherever you are. Some days may require more focus on work, while others demand attention to personal relationships or self-care. Balance is dynamic, constantly shifting based on your current needs.

Rather than striving for perfection, aim for alignment—where your actions reflect your values and priorities, even when life feels off-kilter. A busy season at work may require longer hours, but if your core values include family time, make intentional moments to connect, even briefly.

The Power of Saying No
One of the most effective ways to achieve work-life balance is by learning to say no—a simple, yet powerful act. Many of us overextend ourselves by saying yes to too many things, leaving little room for what truly matters. Every time you say no to something that's out of alignment with your priorities, you create space for what's essential.

Saying no isn't selfish—it's intentional. It's a way of protecting your time, energy, and well-being. Remember, you can't pour from an empty cup. By setting boundaries and focusing on what matters most, you're better able to show up fully for both work and personal life.

Work-Life Balance as a Season, Not a Destination
Balance isn't a goal you reach—it's a seasonal ebb and flow. Think of life as a garden: some areas will bloom while others need pruning. Work-life balance means adjusting your efforts as life's seasons shift. During times of intense work, give yourself permission to pause and recharge when needed. During quieter seasons, lean into relationships, hobbies, and self-care.

Instead of chasing perfect balance, embrace the rhythm of life—some days will feel chaotic, while others will feel peaceful. The key is to remain intentional, knowing when to push forward and when to step back.

Balance is About Presence and Priorities
Achieving work-life balance means recognizing which parts of your life are the glass balls—the non-negotiables that must be handled with care. It's about saying no to distractions that don't align with your priorities and embracing the shifting nature of life. Balance is not about being perfect—it's about being present and honoring what matters most.

Section 2: Boundaries and Burnout Prevention – Protecting Your Energy

The Role of Boundaries in Balance
One of the greatest challenges in achieving work-life balance is

knowing where to draw the line. Without boundaries, work, responsibilities, and obligations tend to creep into every corner of life, leaving little space for rest or joy. Healthy boundaries are the guardrails that protect your time, energy, and mental well-being.

Setting boundaries isn't about being rigid—it's about being intentional with your resources. Saying no to something that drains you or doesn't align with your values allows you to say yes to what truly matters. Boundaries are an act of self-respect and a necessary tool for avoiding burnout.

A close friend once took on every project at work, thinking it was the key to career success. She said yes to every request, every late meeting, and every task, believing that her hard work would eventually be noticed. But instead of recognition, she found herself exhausted and burned out. After hitting rock bottom, she finally learned to say no, set clear boundaries, and prioritize self-care. The difference was immediate—her energy returned, and so did her passion for her work.

How to Set Boundaries Without Guilt

Many people struggle with setting boundaries because they fear disappointing others or being seen as selfish. But setting boundaries isn't selfish—it's an essential act of self-care. Here are ways to set boundaries effectively:

- Communicate Clearly: Be upfront about your limits. For example, let colleagues know when you are unavailable after work hours.
- Start Small: Set boundaries in small ways—like designating certain times as "unavailable" periods—and build confidence over time.

- Stay Firm: Boundaries lose their effectiveness when they aren't honored. Be consistent in maintaining the limits you set.
- Release Guilt: Understand that prioritizing your well-being helps you show up better in all areas of life.

Burnout Prevention: Rest as a Non-Negotiable
Burnout often creeps in when rest takes a back seat to productivity. We live in a culture that glorifies busyness, but the truth is, rest is essential for sustained success. The more you give yourself permission to rest, the more energy you'll have to give back.

Practical strategies for avoiding burnout:

1. Schedule Downtime: Treat rest like any other important appointment—block it off on your calendar.
2. Learn to Disconnect: Build tech-free moments into your day to recharge.
3. Delegate When Possible: Not everything needs to be done by you—ask for help when needed.
4. Check-in with Yourself Regularly: Pause throughout your day and ask yourself: *Am I moving in alignment with my priorities?*

Boundaries Are the Foundation of Balance
Creating work-life balance isn't about doing everything perfectly—it's about setting clear boundaries that allow room for rest, reflection, and joy. Burnout happens when boundaries aren't respected and rest is sacrificed for productivity. By learning to say no and building in moments of rest, you protect your energy

and ensure that you can show up fully for the things that matter most.

Section 3: Energy Alignment – Living by Design, Not Default

Rather than focusing on flow and perfection, we'll zoom in on intentional energy alignment—how you consciously design your days to match your energy with your priorities.

Designing Life with Energy in Mind

Think of your energy as a currency—you only have a limited amount to spend each day. Work-life balance isn't just about managing your time; it's about investing your energy into the things that matter most. When you spend your energy intentionally, life feels less draining and more aligned with your values.

Many people live on autopilot, responding to life's demands without pausing to ask: Where do I want my energy to go? But intentional living requires designing your day in a way that honors your personal rhythm—knowing when to push forward and when to rest.

Energy Cycles and Prioritization

Each of us has unique energy cycles—times during the day when we're at our best and moments when we need to recharge. Rather than forcing productivity, align your tasks with your natural rhythm. If you're most creative in the morning, reserve that time for brainstorming or deep work. If your energy dips in the afternoon, schedule lighter activities or breaks.

Practical Strategies for Energy Alignment

1. Morning Check-ins: Start your day by asking, *What deserves my best energy today?*
2. Batching Energy-Intensive Tasks: Reserve high-energy moments for deep, focused work.
3. Create Energy Rest Stops: Build intentional pauses throughout your day to refuel, such as mindful breathing or a short walk.
4. End-of-Day Reflection: Ask yourself, *Did I invest my energy where it mattered today?* If not, adjust for tomorrow.

The Danger of Living on Autopilot
Many people go through life reacting to whatever comes their way—emails, requests, meetings—without pausing to realign their actions with what's important. Living intentionally means responding thoughtfully rather than reacting impulsively. It's about knowing where your energy is going and making conscious adjustments when needed.

Align Energy with Purpose
When you align your energy with your priorities, life feels more intentional and less chaotic. Instead of juggling everything at once, you focus on what truly matters, making sure your actions reflect your values. The goal isn't to get it all done—it's to invest your energy in ways that make a lasting impact.

Section 4: The Story – The Juggler and the Glass Balls

In a bustling city, a renowned juggler named Matteo was the star of every street performance. Crowds gathered to watch him juggle more objects than anyone could imagine—shining balls, fruits, flaming torches, even random objects tossed from the audience.

Matteo took pride in his ability to juggle it all, believing that more was better. Every day, he pushed himself harder, adding more objects to his act. But with each performance, the weight of the responsibility began to grow heavier. Matteo felt overwhelmed, yet he couldn't stop—after all, the crowd loved his ability to keep everything in the air.

The Breaking Point
One morning, Matteo noticed something troubling: his favorite glass ball had cracked. It was the most precious of his objects—a delicate orb that symbolized his most important relationships and personal well-being. In the pursuit of juggling everything, he had neglected what mattered most.

The juggler tried to ignore the crack, thinking, I'll fix it later. But that day never came. And before long, the glass ball shattered, slipping through his fingers mid-performance and crashing to the ground. The crowd gasped, but Matteo's heart sank deeper—because this was the one ball he couldn't replace.

As Matteo stared at the shattered glass ball, he felt a wave of clarity wash over him. For the first time, he understood that juggling more didn't mean success. It meant distraction. Peace came when he realized he didn't need to catch everything—he just needed to catch what mattered most. And that meant saying no, even when the crowd cheered for more.

The Lesson of the Juggler
Matteo took a step back from performing and reflected on his life. He realized that not every ball he juggled was made of glass.

Some were rubber—they could bounce back if dropped. But others, like the glass ball, represented his closest relationships, health, and well-being—things that, if broken, couldn't be restored easily.

This realization transformed Matteo's approach. He stopped juggling more just for the sake of it and started prioritizing the objects that mattered most. He kept a few important glass balls in the air, ensuring they were always given the care they deserved.

And when someone tossed a new object into his act, Matteo no longer tried to catch everything—he learned to say no to things that didn't align with his values.

The New Rhythm of Life
Matteo returned to performing, but this time, his act looked different. He juggled fewer objects but with greater precision and joy. The audience still cheered, but what mattered more to Matteo was the peace he found in knowing he wasn't dropping the things that mattered most.

The juggler's story teaches us that life isn't about keeping everything in the air—it's about knowing which balls to hold onto and which ones to let go. Some things will bounce back, but others require our full attention and care.

Focus on What Matters
The story of Matteo reminds us that not everything demands equal effort. True balance comes from recognizing what's essential and letting go of the rest. When we focus on what

matters most—our relationships, health, and purpose—we create a rhythm that feels sustainable and fulfilling.

Life isn't about juggling it all; it's about knowing which things are too precious to drop.

Section 5: Leadership in Balance – Living with Intention and Purpose

True work-life balance isn't about **juggling everything perfectly**; it's about **aligning your actions** with your values and creating a life that reflects what matters most. Leaders who embrace this mindset don't just achieve success—they inspire others to **pursue meaningful lives** as well.

Living by Example
People are more likely to follow those who live intentionally—leaders whose personal and professional lives reflect their core beliefs. Living with purpose means knowing when to push forward and when to rest, when to say yes to opportunities and when to let go of things that no longer serve your vision.

When leaders embrace balance, they model the idea that success isn't about constant productivity—it's about being fully present in whatever you choose to do. This encourages others to find their own rhythm rather than chase unrealistic expectations.

The Ripple Effect of Balanced Leadership
Balanced leadership isn't just personal—it creates a ripple effect that impacts families, teams, and communities. Leaders who live with intention inspire others to do the same, building cultures of trust, empathy, and sustainable success. When people feel

empowered to balance their lives, they become more engaged, creative, and resilient.

Aligning Actions with Values
At the heart of balanced leadership is alignment—making sure your daily actions reflect your long-term values. This alignment allows you to say yes to the right things and no to the distractions that pull you away from your purpose. It's not about doing everything—it's about doing what matters most.

The Legacy of Balance
The impact of balanced leadership extends far beyond individual success. It leaves behind a legacy of growth and empowerment—a blueprint for others to follow. As **Lao Tzu** wisely said: **"A leader is best when people barely know he exists; when his work is done, his aim fulfilled, they will say: we did it ourselves."**

When leaders live with balance, they create environments where people thrive—not because they are told what to do, but because they feel empowered to lead themselves.

Balance as a Leadership Legacy
Leadership isn't just about guiding others—it's about living with integrity and purpose, inspiring others to do the same. When you embrace balance, you create a legacy of intentional living that outlasts titles and achievements. The real measure of success lies not in what you accomplish alone, but in the lives you touch and empower along the way

Chapter 12: Financial Wellbeing and Success

Section 1: Redefining Wealth – Aligning Money with Meaning

**Too many people spend money they earned... to buy things they don't want... to impress people that they don't like."
—Will Rogers**

When most people think of wealth, they picture bank accounts, investments, or luxury lifestyles. But financial well-being is about much more than accumulating money—it's about living intentionally and using resources to build a meaningful life. True wealth isn't just about having more; it's about having enough to align with your purpose and values.

Wealth without purpose feels like a bottomless chase for more, while aligning your finances with your values turns each dollar into a building block for a life well-lived.

Reimagining Financial Freedom – From Fear to Purpose
Many of us grew up with scarcity mindsets, believing that money is something to chase, hold onto tightly, or fear losing. But financial well-being begins with a shift in mindset—from scarcity to abundance. Abundance doesn't mean extravagance; it means trusting that you can create opportunities, make wise decisions, and attract the resources you need to thrive.

Abundance asks us to view money not as an end but as a tool for freedom—freedom to pursue what matters, support others, and live in alignment with our values. This mindset shift opens the door to financial choices based on purpose rather than fear.

Defining Your Financial Values
Just as we align actions with personal values, financial well-being comes from aligning your money decisions with your core values. What do you want your money to say about the life you're building? Does it reflect freedom, generosity, security, or growth?

Here's a quick exercise to start:

- Identify your top three financial values. Examples: freedom, adventure, stability, giving.
- Audit your recent spending: Does your spending align with these values? If not, what small changes could bring them into alignment?

The goal isn't to restrict yourself—it's to ensure your financial choices reflect the life you truly want.

Money as a Means, Not the Goal
Money, by itself, doesn't bring meaning—it's the purpose behind the money that gives it power. Financial success is about using resources wisely to support your vision. Whether that means saving for freedom, investing in personal growth, or giving generously to causes you care about, every financial decision becomes an opportunity to align with purpose.

Rather than chasing wealth for its own sake, financial well-being asks:

- How can my financial habits reflect my values?
- What does financial freedom mean to me?
- How can I use money to create a meaningful impact?

This approach ensures that every dollar serves a higher purpose, bringing you closer to a life of fulfillment and balance.

The Role of Gratitude in Financial Success
Gratitude is a powerful practice that shifts your focus from what you lack to what you have. This shift cultivates financial contentment—the ability to appreciate your current resources while striving for more.

Try This:

- Daily gratitude journaling: Write down one thing you appreciate about your financial situation each day, whether it's a small savings habit or a supportive financial relationship.

- Celebrate small wins: Acknowledge each step toward financial well-being—whether it's paying off debt, creating a budget, or saving for a future goal.

Gratitude helps you stay motivated while building wealth, ensuring you feel fulfilled along the way.

Wealth Aligned with Purpose
Financial success isn't about how much you accumulate—it's about how aligned your resources are with your values and goals. When you shift from a scarcity mindset to an abundance perspective, money becomes a tool for creating freedom and meaning. True wealth lies in the ability to live intentionally, using resources to build a life that reflects your deepest values.

Section 2: Shifting from Scarcity to Abundance – Transforming Mindsets

Many people grow up with a scarcity mindset, believing there is never enough—enough money, resources, or opportunities. This mindset leads to fear, comparison, and a constant chase for security. But financial well-being begins when we shift to an abundance mindset—the belief that opportunities are plentiful and resources can grow through intentional action.

The Power of Perspective – Redefining What's 'Enough'
A scarcity mindset tells us that having more is the key to happiness, yet many people with overflowing bank accounts still feel unfulfilled. In contrast, an abundance mindset focuses on appreciating and growing what you already have. This doesn't mean ignoring ambition—it means recognizing that wealth starts in the mindset you cultivate.

As **Epictetus** reminds us:
"Wealth consists not in having great possessions, but in having few wants."

When we learn to align our desires with our values, we free ourselves from the endless pursuit of more and experience financial freedom—regardless of how much or how little we have.

From Hoarding to Flow – Letting Resources Circulate

People with a scarcity mindset often hoard money, fearing that spending or sharing will leave them with nothing. But true financial well-being involves flow—letting resources circulate in ways that reflect your values. This could mean investing in personal growth, giving generously, or taking thoughtful risks that create future opportunities.

Think of money like water in a stream—it must flow to stay fresh. When you let resources move through your life, whether through investments or generosity, you open yourself to new opportunities. Abundance teaches us that money isn't something to cling to—it's a tool to help us grow and give.

Practical Steps for Shifting to Abundance

- Gratitude practice: Start each day by listing things you appreciate in your financial life, no matter how small. This helps reframe your mindset toward what you have rather than what you lack.
- Invest in growth: Whether it's learning a new skill or saving for the future, use your money in ways that align with your long-term vision.

- Give back regularly: Giving—whether through donations or time—reinforces the idea that resources are plentiful and creates meaningful connections.

Abundance Over Fear
Shifting from scarcity to abundance isn't just about financial strategies—it's about changing the way you see and experience life. With an abundance mindset, money becomes a tool for freedom, growth, and generosity, rather than a source of fear or stress. When you let go of the fear of not having enough, you unlock the ability to create opportunities and live with greater purpose and joy.

Section 3: Aligning Financial Habits with Values – Building Sustainable Success

Financial success isn't just about achieving big milestones—it's about developing consistent habits that align with your values. These daily choices build the foundation for long-term financial well-being. When your habits reflect your values, managing money feels natural and empowering rather than stressful or overwhelming.

The Power of Small, Intentional Habits
Big changes don't happen overnight; they emerge from small, consistent actions. Whether it's setting aside a small amount each week or tracking expenses to stay aware of spending, these seemingly small actions compound over time.

Think of it as planting seeds—each small habit you nurture grows into something meaningful, even if the results aren't visible right away. The goal is to align your financial habits with the life you want to create.

One small business owner committed to setting aside just 5% of every sale for future growth. Over time, that small habit compounded, allowing her to expand her business debt-free and invest in new opportunities.

Examples of Purpose-Driven Habits

- Saving with Meaning: Instead of saving aimlessly, assign your savings a purpose (e.g., an emergency fund for peace of mind or a travel fund for experiences).
- Conscious Spending: Spend on what brings real value to your life, whether it's investing in personal growth, experiences, or relationships.
- Giving with Intention: Make giving a part of your financial routine, whether donating to causes or offering help to those around you.

Creating Systems for Success

To align habits with values, it helps to build simple systems that remove decision fatigue. For example:

- Automatic savings plans ensure you prioritize your financial goals without needing to think about them daily.
- Monthly reviews help you assess progress and realign spending with your values.
- Accountability partners (friends, family, or mentors) offer support and motivation.

These systems ensure that you stay on track, even when life becomes busy or overwhelming.

Trusting the Process of Growth
Aligning habits with values isn't about perfection—it's about progress. There will be setbacks along the way, but each step forward reinforces your commitment to financial well-being. Remember: Success is not an outcome—it's a process.

As **Ayn Rand** reminds us:
"Money is only a tool. It will take you wherever you wish, but it will not replace you as the driver."

This quote captures the essence of value-aligned habits—you are in control of your financial journey, and your habits are the vehicle that moves you toward meaningful success.

Aligning Actions with Purpose
When financial habits reflect your values, every decision feels like an investment in the life you truly want. Small, consistent choices create momentum, making it easier to stay aligned with your long-term goals. Success isn't about how fast you get there—it's about building a sustainable path that supports you every step of the way.

Section 4: The Farmer Who Planted Dreams – A Story of Intentional Wealth

In a small, humble village nestled between rolling hills, lived a farmer named Ravi. Ravi wasn't rich by any standard measure—his land was modest, and his crops were simple. But what made him different was his attitude toward wealth and success. He believed that true wealth wasn't just about harvesting crops but about sowing dreams.

Every season, Ravi would plant a small portion of his fields with something new—an experiment. Sometimes it was flowers he had never grown, and other times it was fruits the locals didn't know could thrive in their region. His neighbors laughed at him, calling him foolish for planting things that didn't guarantee profit. "Why waste good soil on dreams?" they'd say. But Ravi would simply smile and reply, "Every harvest begins with a dream."

A Season of Failure
One year, Ravi's dreams didn't go as planned. The rains came late, and many of his experimental crops withered before they could bloom. His neighbors shook their heads, saying, "We told you not to waste your time." Ravi felt the sting of disappointment but didn't let it take root in his heart. He saw failure not as the end, but as part of the process.

Instead of giving up, he reflected on what went wrong. Maybe the flowers needed more shade, and the fruits needed richer soil. Each failure became a lesson planted for the next season. Ravi knew that growth takes time and patience, just like farming.

The Harvest of Dreams
The following season, Ravi made small adjustments. He planted the flowers in the shade of his fruit trees and enriched the soil with compost. To everyone's surprise, his garden flourished. The flowers bloomed in vibrant colors, attracting visitors from other villages, and his fruits were sweeter than anyone expected.

But Ravi didn't measure success by the flowers he sold or the fruits he harvested. His real wealth came from the joy of learning and experimenting. What he grew wasn't just crops—it was the freedom to dream, to try, and to grow.

The Legacy of Intentional Wealth
Years later, as Ravi sat under the shade of his blooming trees, children from the village would gather around him, curious about his garden. "Why did you plant all these things, even when they failed?" they'd ask.

Ravi would smile and say, "Because wealth isn't about what you have—it's about what you create and who you become along the way. Even when a crop fails, it teaches you something new. And when you plant with purpose, every season brings a harvest—whether it's fruit or wisdom."

The villagers eventually stopped calling Ravi foolish and began planting dreams of their own. His garden became more than a source of food—it became a symbol of growth, abundance, and intention. Ravi's story spread far beyond his village, inspiring others to see wealth not as something to hoard but as a journey of creating, learning, and giving.

The Lesson of the Farmer
Ravi's story teaches us that true wealth is not measured by money alone. It's about living intentionally, planting seeds aligned with your dreams, and embracing both success and failure as part of the journey. Wealth is not just a destination—it's the process of growing into your fullest potential and sharing that growth with others.

Section 5: Legacy of Financial Well-Being – Living with Purpose and Impact

True wealth is not just about personal gain; it's about leaving a lasting legacy. Financial well-being becomes meaningful when it extends beyond our own lives and impacts those around us. A legacy isn't defined by the size of your bank account—it's shaped by the values you live by and the lives you touch.

Consider the story of a teacher who saved modestly throughout her life, and upon retirement, used her savings to establish scholarships for underprivileged students. Her legacy wasn't just in the dollars saved but in the lives she empowered through education.

Creating a Ripple Effect of Impact

Your financial choices today can create ripples that extend far beyond yourself. A well-timed gift, an investment in someone else's growth, or teaching your children how to manage money wisely can have a profound, lasting impact. When aligned with purpose, wealth becomes a tool for empowering others, creating opportunities where none existed before.

Think of the story of Ravi, the farmer—his wealth wasn't measured by what he accumulated, but by the seeds he planted that inspired others to dream and grow. Your legacy isn't just what you leave behind—it's what you cultivate along the way.

Aligning Money with Meaningful Impact

To create a lasting legacy, wealth must align with your core values. Ask yourself:

- What values do I want my financial legacy to reflect?
- Who can benefit from my resources, knowledge, or generosity?
- How can I ensure that my financial habits empower others and align with my vision for the future?

A financial legacy isn't about control—it's about empowerment. The goal isn't to dictate how others use what you leave behind, but to inspire them to live with purpose and intention.

The Power of Living Your Legacy Now
A legacy isn't something you create only at the end of life—it's something you live every day. By aligning your current financial habits with your values, you start building that legacy now. Every choice you make—whether it's saving, spending, giving, or investing—becomes a part of the story you leave behind.

This approach ensures that wealth is not an endpoint but a process—one where financial well-being, generosity, and purpose intersect.

Living a Life Aligned with Abundance
When you view wealth as a tool to create impact and live intentionally, financial well-being becomes a natural part of your life. It's no longer about striving or scarcity—it's about flow, balance, and alignment. True wealth isn't just what you have—it's how you live and the impact you leave on others.

By choosing to live your legacy now, you not only experience the joy of financial freedom but also create a lasting ripple of purpose, meaning, and growth that will continue long after you're gone.

Wealth is about more than accumulation—it's about creating impact and living with purpose. A meaningful financial legacy starts today, with every choice you make. When your financial life aligns with your values, you create a ripple effect of positive change that extends far beyond your lifetime.

Chapter 13: The Journey of Continuous Learning

Section 1: Learning as a Lifelong Journey – Embracing Curiosity and Change

"It is what we know already that often prevents us from learning."
—Claude Bernard

Learning doesn't end when school does—it's a lifelong journey, one that shapes how we grow and evolve. The key to continuous learning isn't just gathering information—it's about developing the ability to adapt and grow with every experience. Life constantly offers lessons, but it's up to us to remain curious and open to learning, even when those lessons come in unexpected ways.

The Importance of Curiosity
Curiosity is the spark that fuels lifelong learning. When you

approach life with a sense of wonder—asking questions, exploring new ideas, and embracing challenges—you unlock the potential to grow. Curiosity keeps your mind open, encouraging you to see beyond what's comfortable and familiar.

For example, think of a successful entrepreneur who regularly seeks out conversations with people from different industries. By staying curious and learning from others, they continually expand their knowledge, fueling innovation.

Think about children—how they explore the world with wide-eyed curiosity, asking endless questions. Somewhere along the way, many of us lose that spark, trading curiosity for routine. But learning begins again when curiosity is rekindled. It's about staying hungry for new knowledge and understanding that every experience holds the potential to teach you something.

Consider someone who, after years in a routine career, decided to pursue a new passion simply out of curiosity. By taking night classes in a completely different field, they not only found fulfillment but unlocked a new career path they never anticipated.

The Value of Embracing Change
Continuous learning goes hand in hand with embracing change. The world is constantly evolving, and those who learn to adapt thrive. Learning isn't just about accumulating knowledge—it's about becoming someone who can navigate change with confidence.

When you embrace learning as a journey, setbacks become opportunities for growth. Failure becomes a lesson, not a stopping point. The ability to adapt, adjust, and stay curious allows you to find meaning in every challenge.

Learning in Everyday Moments
The beauty of lifelong learning is that it doesn't require a classroom or formal setting. Opportunities to learn are woven into the fabric of daily life. Whether it's learning from a conversation, picking up a new hobby, or reflecting on a personal experience, every moment offers insight.

- At the end of each day, ask yourself, What did I learn today?
- Keep a journal of lessons, big or small. It could be something practical or a deeper insight about yourself.
- Celebrate the small moments of learning—those are often the most profound.

The Courage to Stay Open to Learning
Learning requires humility—the willingness to admit that you don't know everything and the courage to explore the unknown. It's okay to be a beginner. In fact, the best learners are those who remain students throughout life, never feeling they've "arrived."

The poet **Rumi** said it best:
"Try not to resist the changes that come your way. Instead, let life live through you. And do not worry that your life is turning upside down. How do you know that the side you are used to is better than the one to come?"

This quote captures the heart of continuous learning—the courage to welcome change, uncertainty, and the unknown as opportunities for growth.

Key Takeaway: Curiosity and Change as Learning Catalysts
Lifelong learning is about more than acquiring knowledge—it's about staying curious, embracing change, and being open to the lessons life offers. With each new experience, you grow not only in knowledge but also in wisdom. When you live with curiosity and adaptability, every step becomes part of a meaningful learning journey.

Section 2: Learning Through Action – Turning Knowledge into Wisdom

Many people assume that learning happens solely through books, courses, or lectures. But true learning is more than the accumulation of knowledge—it's about applying what you've learned. Learning without action is like collecting seeds and never planting them. To grow, you must put what you've gathered into practice.

From Knowledge to Wisdom
Knowledge gives you information; wisdom shows you how to apply it meaningfully. Think of someone who reads countless books on fitness but never exercises. The information they've gathered holds potential, but until they act, that potential remains unrealized. Wisdom comes from experiencing and experimenting, from applying lessons and refining them through practice.

Every time you apply what you learn—whether in relationships, at work, or through personal habits—you transform knowledge into wisdom. Learning through action creates depth and helps lessons stick. Mistakes become part of the learning process, offering insights you couldn't get from theory alone.

Wisdom not only guides your actions but shapes how you approach challenges and decisions, allowing you to navigate life with greater clarity and purpose.

Reflection as Part of the Process
Action is essential, but so is reflection. Taking time to pause and reflect allows you to see what worked, what didn't, and how to improve moving forward. Reflection is the bridge between experience and growth. Without it, you risk repeating the same mistakes or missing the deeper lessons hidden within your actions

- Daily Reflection: At the end of each day, write down one action you took and what you learned from it.
- Growth Journaling: Track areas where you want to improve, noting what actions brought progress and what didn't.

This habit helps turn action into wisdom, ensuring every step forward adds to your growth.

Learning as an Evolving Process
The beauty of learning through action is that it's evolving and continuous. Even when you think you've mastered a skill, new challenges will emerge that force you to refine your approach. This process keeps you humble and curious, knowing there's always more to learn.

You never "arrive" at the end of learning—each experience offers new insights, no matter how small. This mindset ensures that learning becomes a lifelong journey, keeping your mind and skills fresh and adaptable.

The Courage to Learn Through Failure
One of the greatest obstacles to learning through action is the fear of failure. Many people hesitate to act because they fear getting things wrong. But failure isn't the opposite of learning—it's part of it. Each failure brings with it new understanding, revealing what works and what doesn't.

As **William Butler Yeats** put it:
"Education is not the filling of a pail, but the lighting of a fire."

This quote reminds us that learning comes from engaging with the process—from trying, failing, and refining. Perfection isn't the goal—progress is.

Learning through action transforms information into wisdom. When you apply what you learn, reflect on your experiences, and embrace failure as part of the process, growth becomes continuous. The journey of learning doesn't end—it evolves, creating wisdom that shapes who you are becoming.

Section 3: Expanding the Learning Horizon – Unlearning, Curiosity, and Mastery through Practice

As we discussed earlier in Chapter 2, adopting a growth mindset is crucial for personal growth—it helps us embrace challenges and view failure as a stepping stone. Here we will revisit Growth and Fixed mindset again, before we move.

Shifting from Fixed to Growth Mindset
A growth mindset is the belief that abilities, intelligence, and skills can be developed through effort, learning, and persistence.

It's the mindset that fuels continuous learning, allowing you to see challenges not as roadblocks but as opportunities for growth.

People with a fixed mindset believe that talent and intelligence are innate—something you either have or you don't. This mindset creates fear of failure, as any setback is seen as proof of inadequacy. But with a growth mindset, challenges become part of the learning journey. Mistakes and failures aren't indicators of limits; they're stepping stones toward growth.

Adopting a growth mindset requires reframing challenges as invitations to improve. Instead of thinking, "I'm just not good at this," the growth mindset encourages you to say, "I'm not good at this yet."

A growth mindset allows you to embrace challenges as opportunities to learn and grow. With effort, feedback, and resilience, learning becomes a continuous journey of self-improvement. By shifting from a fixed mindset to a growth mindset, you unlock your full potential, transforming obstacles into stepping stones toward lifelong learning.

However, learning doesn't stop with how we frame challenges—it also involves unlearning what no longer serves us, staying curious, and mastering new skills through intentional practice. These are the keys to continuous growth in an ever-changing world.

The Power of Unlearning
True learning isn't just about adding new knowledge—it often involves letting go of outdated beliefs and habits that no longer

serve us. This process of unlearning is essential for making space for fresh ideas and perspectives.

Think of it like upgrading software—before installing new updates, you need to remove the old versions that no longer work efficiently. The same applies to learning: sometimes, the hardest lesson is realizing that what you thought you knew is no longer relevant.

Unlearning takes courage, as it challenges the comfort of familiarity. But in today's world, where knowledge evolves rapidly, the ability to unlearn and adapt is what keeps us growing.

For instance, think of a veteran engineer who had to unlearn old manufacturing techniques to adapt to the rise of automation. By letting go of the familiar and embracing new technologies, they stayed relevant and continued to innovate.

Learning Through Curiosity – The Spark of Discovery
Curiosity is the engine of learning. When we're curious, learning becomes effortless because we're motivated by the joy of discovery. Whether it's trying out a new hobby, exploring a different culture, or diving into an unfamiliar topic, curiosity keeps our minds open to new possibilities.

Curiosity-driven learning isn't about achieving specific outcomes—it's about embracing the process of exploration. It encourages us to ask questions, seek out different perspectives, and remain open to ideas that challenge our assumptions.
Practical tip:

- Practice "What if?" questions: Use curiosity to reframe your thinking by asking, "What if I tried this differently?" or "What would happen if I explored this idea further?"

Mastery Through Practice – The Art of Repetition
While curiosity fuels exploration, mastery comes from practice. To develop expertise, we need to engage in intentional, repeated effort over time. The path to mastery isn't glamorous—it's often marked by tedious repetition and small, incremental improvements.

Take **Bruce Lee**, who famously said, **'I fear not the man who has practiced 10,000 kicks once, but I fear the man who has practiced one kick 10,000 times.'** His success came from relentlessly mastering the basics through constant practice.

Think of a musician practicing scales daily or an athlete refining their form. These individuals understand that skill-building requires patience and dedication. Mastery is not achieved overnight—it's cultivated through consistent practice, even when progress feels slow.

- Break big goals into micro-practices: Focus on small, achievable actions each day to build momentum. Over time, these practices accumulate, leading to significant growth.

Lifelong learning isn't just about acquiring new knowledge—it's about unlearning old habits, nurturing curiosity, and practicing with intention. These approaches keep us adaptable, engaged, and always growing. When we embrace all forms of learning—

whether through exploration, reflection, or repetition—we unlock the full potential of continuous growth.

Section 4: The Story – The Librarian Who Stopped Reading

In a quiet town nestled between rolling hills, there lived a librarian named Eleanor. For decades, she devoted herself to books, organizing countless volumes and guiding readers on their literary journeys. Her life revolved around knowledge—cataloging it, recommending it, and absorbing it herself. Eleanor had read everything, from philosophy to fiction, history to science. Yet, despite all her reading, she began to feel as though something was missing.

One rainy afternoon, while shelving yet another new release, Eleanor paused and whispered to herself, "What's the point of all this knowledge if it never leaves the pages?" It was a thought that had been lingering for months—a gnawing feeling that simply knowing was no longer enough.

The Shift from Knowing to Experiencing

That day, Eleanor made an unusual decision: she would stop reading. Not forever, but just for a while. Instead of burying herself in books, she would begin living the things she'd read about for so many years. She closed the library early, packed a small bag, and set off to experience life firsthand.

In the following months, Eleanor embarked on small adventures. She visited nearby farms to learn how food is grown, hiked through the forests she'd only read about in travel books, and spent time with artists, understanding their creative processes. She even volunteered at a local community center, applying leadership principles she had once studied in management books.

Each new experience taught Eleanor something that no book ever could—the beauty of doing, feeling, and connecting. She realized that knowledge on its own is incomplete without action and engagement.

Bridging Knowledge and Action
Eleanor's journey didn't mean she gave up on reading forever. Books still held an important place in her life, but now they served as starting points rather than destinations. Instead of passively consuming knowledge, she actively applied what she learned.

When she returned to the library months later, Eleanor began offering new kinds of programs—story circles where people shared personal experiences, hands-on workshops where learning happened through doing, and community projects where knowledge and action came together. The library became a hub for growth, not just through reading, but through living.

Eleanor's story reminds us that learning is more than gathering information—it's about applying what we know, experimenting, and allowing knowledge to shape how we live. True wisdom comes not just from reading books but from engaging with life.

The Key Lesson
Lifelong learning is about more than accumulating knowledge—it's about integrating what you learn into your daily actions and experiences. Just like Eleanor, we must find ways to apply what we know and turn theory into practice.Learning becomes

meaningful when it informs how we show up in the world, how we interact with others, and how we grow through experience.

This story teaches us that books can guide us, but **living** is where real learning happens.

Section 5: Learning as a Lifelong Practice – Growth Without Limits

Lifelong learning isn't just about formal education or mastering a single skill—it's about cultivating a mindset that welcomes continuous growth. It's the recognition that every moment offers an opportunity to learn, whether through successes, failures, or unexpected challenges. The goal is not to arrive at a destination of knowledge but to remain open, curious, and engaged throughout life.

The most beautiful aspect of lifelong learning is that there is always something new to discover, no matter how much you've already learned. Each day offers a new opportunity to evolve, reminding us that growth truly has no end.

The Practice of Staying Curious

Curiosity is the foundation of lifelong learning. When you approach life with curiosity, the world becomes a classroom, and every experience a lesson. Curiosity invites you to ask questions, explore new interests, and step outside of your comfort zone. It's not about having all the answers—it's about enjoying the process of discovery.

Rather than seeing learning as something confined to books or classes, view it as an everyday practice. It's in conversations with strangers, new hobbies, and even moments of quiet reflection. A curious mindset allows you to find meaning in the ordinary and turn small experiences into meaningful insights.

Learning Through Action
True learning happens when knowledge translates into action. Whether it's experimenting with a new idea, testing a skill in real life, or reflecting on a mistake, learning requires more than passive consumption—it demands engagement. Every step forward, even the missteps, contributes to your growth.

Think of learning like planting seeds. Each new skill, insight, or experience is a seed that grows over time through action and reflection. Not every seed will sprout immediately, but with patience and persistence, growth will come.

The Power of Reflection
In our fast-paced world, it's easy to move from one task to the next without pausing to reflect. But reflection is a vital part of lifelong learning. It helps you make sense of your experiences, extract lessons from challenges, and reinforce progress.

- Daily Reflection Practice: At the end of each day, take five minutes to ask yourself: What did I learn today? What challenged me? What can I do differently tomorrow?

Reflection creates a feedback loop that strengthens your learning. It turns experience into wisdom and helps you grow more intentional with each passing day.

The Gift of Lifelong Learning
One of the greatest gifts of lifelong learning is the sense of renewal it brings. No matter where you are in life, there is always

room to grow. Learning keeps you engaged, connected, and open to new possibilities. It reminds you that life is not a series of fixed outcomes but a journey of continuous evolution.

The beauty of this practice is that it's available to everyone—regardless of age, background, or circumstances. It's about embracing growth as a way of life, knowing that each step forward, no matter how small, is part of your journey.

As **Albert Einstein** said, **'Once you stop learning, you start dying.'** Lifelong learning keeps us vibrant, curious, and ever-growing, allowing us to embrace life's endless opportunities for growth."

Growth is a Lifelong Journey
Lifelong learning isn't a race with a finish line—it's a mindset that embraces growth at every stage of life. It's about staying curious, turning knowledge into action, and reflecting on your experiences. This practice allows you to adapt, evolve, and find meaning in the everyday moments.

When you commit to lifelong learning, you give yourself the freedom to grow without limits. Every lesson, every mistake, and every new experience becomes a stepping stone on your journey. Learning isn't just something you do—it's who you become.

Chapter 14: The Digital Age and Personal Growth

Section 1: Mindful Engagement – Navigating Technology with Purpose

We live in a world that's always connected. Notifications buzz, emails arrive at all hours, and social media feeds scroll endlessly. While technology offers incredible tools for connection, learning, and productivity, it can also pull us in too many directions at once. The key to thriving in this hyperconnected world lies not in rejecting technology, but in engaging with it mindfully.

The Myth of Multitasking
Many believe that juggling multiple tasks makes them more efficient. But research shows that multitasking drains energy and reduces focus. Each time we switch between tasks, we lose a bit of attention, creating mental clutter. True productivity comes from

single-tasking—immersing yourself fully in one task before moving to the next.

Consider a writer who sets intentional boundaries by turning off notifications during their creative work hours. By doing so, they preserve their mental space for deep work, allowing technology to serve them instead of pulling them into distractions.

The Hidden Cost of Distractions
Distractions may seem small, but they come with an unseen price. Studies show that each time your focus is interrupted, it can take 15 to 25 minutes to fully regain your original level of concentration. This phenomenon, known as attention residue, makes it harder to complete tasks efficiently and adds to mental fatigue.

By reducing unnecessary interruptions—like constant notifications or mindless scrolling—you can protect your attention and stay engaged in meaningful work. The fewer distractions you allow, the more momentum you build, creating a smoother, more productive flow.

Setting Digital Boundaries
Technology makes it tempting to be available 24/7, but constant connectivity leads to burnout. Creating intentional boundaries helps you regain control over your time and energy. This might mean:

- Turning off notifications during certain hours.
- Setting limits on screen time for social media.
- Designating tech-free zones—like the dinner table or bedroom.

Boundaries aren't about limiting yourself—they're about prioritizing what matters. When you're intentional about when and how you use technology, you can engage with it meaningfully rather than mindlessly.

Shifting from Consumption to Creation
Technology offers endless opportunities for passive consumption, but the real power lies in using it to create. Whether it's sharing your ideas, building a project, or learning new skills, shifting from consumption to creation allows you to use technology as a tool for personal growth.

Consider this: the time you spend scrolling through feeds could be time spent writing, designing, or building something that aligns with your goals. The choice isn't between using technology or not—it's about how you use it.

Section 2: Digital Minimalism – Decluttering Your Online Life

In a world where every app and platform competes for your attention, digital minimalism offers a way to reclaim control over how you engage with technology. It's not about abandoning technology entirely—it's about being intentional with how you use it, focusing on what adds value and eliminating what doesn't.

The Cost of Digital Clutter
Just like physical clutter drains energy, digital clutter—in the form of unused apps, endless notifications, and overwhelming inboxes—can drain your focus and well-being. Every distraction comes at a cost, pulling you away from meaningful tasks and experiences. Digital minimalism is about recognizing those

hidden costs and making conscious choices about what stays and what goes.

Ask yourself: Is my digital environment supporting or distracting me from my goals? What small steps can I take today to declutter my online life and create more mental space?

Curating Your Digital Environment
Here are some practical ways to start your digital decluttering journey:

- Audit your apps: Remove any that no longer serve a purpose or align with your goals.
- Organize your inbox: Use filters and unsubscribe from unnecessary emails.
- Limit notifications: Only allow essential alerts to maintain focus throughout your day.

These small actions create mental space, giving you room to engage deeply with what truly matters.

Prioritizing Quality Over Quantity
With technology, more isn't always better. Having hundreds of social media connections means little if the interactions lack depth. Digital minimalism encourages focusing on fewer, more meaningful interactions—both online and offline.

Rather than spreading yourself thin across multiple platforms, focus your energy on spaces where you find genuine connection and purpose. This shift from quantity to quality ensures that your time online is well spent.

Intentional Breaks for Reconnection
Taking regular breaks from technology isn't a sign of weakness—it's a strategy for recalibrating your mind and emotions. Whether it's a daily pause from social media or a weekend digital detox, intentional breaks allow you to reconnect with yourself, your relationships, and your goals.

Section 3: Mindful Engagement – Using Technology with Purpose

Technology itself isn't the problem—it's how we engage with it. The goal isn't to abandon the digital world but to interact with it consciously and purposefully. Mindful engagement is about recognizing when technology adds value and when it detracts from what matters most.

Shifting from Passive to Active Use
We often engage with technology passively—scrolling through feeds or checking emails without intention. Mindful engagement flips that script, encouraging you to use technology deliberately, focusing on tasks and activities that align with your values and goals.

For example:

- Instead of endlessly scrolling social media, connect meaningfully with a few people by sending thoughtful messages.
- Use technology for learning and growth—listen to podcasts, take online courses, or read articles that expand your knowledge.

- Replace reactive checking of your phone with scheduled time blocks for digital interactions.

The goal is not to be anti-technology but to choose technology that supports, not controls, your life.

The Role of Intentional Boundaries
Creating boundaries around technology prevents it from taking over your life. Time limits on social media, phone-free spaces, or digital-free hours in the morning or evening give your mind time to rest and recharge.

Practical Boundaries for Mindful Engagement:

- Morning routine without screens: Start your day with journaling or meditation before checking your phone.
- Technology-free meals: Focus on conversation and connection during meals instead of checking devices.
- Set a "digital sunset": Turn off screens an hour before bed to support restful sleep and mental clarity.

Engaging with Technology as a Tool, Not a Trap

Technology is meant to enhance your life, not trap you in cycles of distraction. By setting boundaries and engaging mindfully, you regain control over how you use technology. This empowers you to harness digital tools for meaningful goals—whether it's pursuing creative projects, nurturing relationships, or expanding your knowledge.

Section 4: The Monk Who Loved Technology – A Modern Parable

In a small monastery perched on a mountaintop, lived a monk named Tenzin. Known for his wisdom and simplicity, Tenzin spent his days meditating, tending to the garden, and offering guidance to those who sought it. The world beyond the mountains moved fast, but the rhythm of Tenzin's life remained steady, grounded in the traditions passed down through generations.

One day, a young traveler arrived, clutching a tablet and phone. Intrigued by Tenzin's wisdom, the traveler asked, "Master, how can I escape the chaos of the digital world? Everywhere I go, people are glued to their devices, and I feel lost in the noise."

Tenzin smiled. "Why escape it?" he asked. "Why not learn to live with it?"

The traveler was puzzled. "But how can technology and mindfulness coexist?"

Tenzin leaned forward, his eyes sparkling with humor. "Technology is like fire. It can warm your home or burn it down— it depends on how you use it."

Technology as a Tool, Not a Master
Tenzin shared how, even in the monastery, he used technology— not as a distraction but as a bridge. He read digital texts to deepen his knowledge, connected with distant friends through video calls, and tracked the moon cycles with an app to guide his planting. "You see," he said, "it's not technology that disturbs our peace—it's how we engage with it."

The traveler listened intently, realizing that Tenzin's relationship with technology was not one of avoidance but mastery. The monk didn't let his devices dictate his life; he used them with purpose, always aware of when to engage and when to let go.

Balancing Connection and Solitude
Tenzin's day had boundaries—times for silence and times for connection. When the sun set, he put away his phone and embraced the night in quiet contemplation. "There is a time for everything," he explained. "A time to be connected to the world, and a time to reconnect with yourself."

The traveler understood then that technology wasn't the enemy—it was a tool, and like any tool, its value depended on how it was used. Tenzin had mastered the art of being fully present, whether with a digital device or in silent meditation.

"Remember," Tenzin said, "you don't have to renounce the world to find peace. Just use what serves you, and let go of the rest."

The traveler left the monastery, his heart lighter and his mind clearer. He no longer felt the need to escape technology; instead, he resolved to engage with it thoughtfully, as Tenzin had taught him—using it to enrich his life, not control it.

As the traveler descended from the mountaintop, he realized that his relationship with technology had shifted. It was no longer something to escape from, but something to master—with intention, balance, and clarity.

Section 5: Envisioning a Balanced Digital Future

The digital world isn't going anywhere. With each passing year, technology becomes more deeply woven into the fabric of our lives. The key to thriving in this modern age isn't about escaping the digital realm—it's about crafting a relationship with technology that empowers personal growth, creativity, and meaningful connections.

Aligning Technology with Purpose
Think of technology as an extension of your intentions. Just as you align your actions with your values, your use of technology can also reflect what matters most. Are your apps supporting your learning, creativity, or well-being? Or are they simply filling time with noise?

Tenzin's story reminds us that mastery comes through intention. A simple but powerful way to maintain this alignment is to regularly ask: "Is this adding value to my life or taking me away from it?"

When technology serves your purpose, it becomes a tool for growth. But when it becomes a source of distraction, it's time to step back and recalibrate. The balance lies in knowing when to engage and when to disconnect.

Creating Digital Boundaries
The ability to disconnect is just as important as the ability to connect. Establishing boundaries with technology helps maintain focus, creativity, and mental well-being. Here are a few guiding practices:

- Designate tech-free zones: Keep certain spaces, like the bedroom or dining table, free of devices.
- Set intentional time limits: Schedule moments throughout the day to check messages, but stay present during other activities.

- Practice digital sabbaths: Take occasional breaks from screens to reset your mind and reconnect with yourself or nature.

These boundaries ensure that technology remains a supportive tool, rather than a constant interruption.

Building a Legacy of Digital Mindfulness
The way you engage with technology sets an example for those around you—friends, family, and even future generations. Just as the traveler learned from Tenzin, your mindful use of technology can inspire others to build healthier digital habits. The ripple effect of digital mindfulness spreads through small acts, creating a culture that prioritizes presence over distraction.

Think of it like planting seeds. Each intentional action—whether it's choosing to focus on a meaningful project instead of scrolling aimlessly or having a device-free dinner with loved ones—plants a seed for a more balanced future.

The Future is Yours to Shape
In the end, the relationship between humans and technology isn't fixed—it's evolving, just like everything else. And you have the power to shape that evolution through the choices you make each day. Technology can either be a tool for distraction or a gateway to deeper creativity, learning, and connection. The choice is yours.

As Tenzin said, "Use what serves you, and let go of the rest." With this mindset, you can navigate the digital age with intention, finding harmony between connection and solitude, action and stillness. This balance isn't just a skill—it's a way of life, one that empowers you to thrive in a world that never stops moving.

Chapter 15: Envisioning and Realizing Your Future

Section 1: The Power of Vision – Dreaming with Purpose

"The best way to predict the future is to create it." — Abraham Lincoln

Every great achievement starts with a vision—a clear, compelling picture of the life you want to build. But vision is not just about dreams or daydreaming; it's about intentional clarity and emotional resonance. A powerful vision draws from your deepest values and connects with your sense of purpose, offering a framework that guides you even through moments of uncertainty.

Think of vision as a lighthouse that illuminates your path when the waters get rough. It doesn't eliminate obstacles but ensures you stay on course. This is why having a well-defined vision is more than just a luxury—it becomes essential in navigating the chaos and unpredictability of life.

Take a moment to close your eyes and imagine your ideal future in vivid detail. Picture what you're doing, how you feel, and who's with you. Now, identify one small action you can take today that brings you one step closer to that vision.

The Bridge Between Imagination and Reality
Creating a vision bridges the gap between what is and what could be. Too often, people hesitate to dream big, fearing failure or thinking they don't deserve more. But vision isn't about being "realistic." It's about expanding your horizon—allowing yourself to imagine new possibilities and align your life with them.

Practical visioning isn't passive; it demands both imagination and action. When you anchor your vision with purpose, you stop drifting through life and start making deliberate choices that pull you closer to your future. Even small steps become meaningful because they contribute to something larger than today's challenges.

Reverse-Engineering Your Future
The most effective visions work backward—start by picturing the ideal outcome and trace it back to what needs to happen today to move closer to it. Ask yourself:

- What does my ideal day look like in five years?
- What habits, routines, or systems will help me align with this future?
- What small actions can I take today that reflect the life I want to create?

By reverse-engineering your future, you turn a seemingly distant goal into a series of actionable steps. These steps, though small, gain momentum over time, creating a path toward your envisioned life.

The Emotional Anchor of Vision
A vision isn't just a mental blueprint—it's an emotional anchor. When you connect deeply with your vision, it becomes easier to stay motivated, even when life gets challenging. You're not just pursuing a vague dream; you're working toward something that resonates with your values and brings meaning to your actions.

Athletes visualize their performance before every game. Entrepreneurs envision their success through setbacks. Visionary leaders align their daily decisions with the future they want to create. They all understand this: a clear vision keeps you grounded, even when everything else feels uncertain.

Creating Mental Rehearsals
Incorporate mental rehearsals into your routine—visualizing yourself overcoming obstacles and making progress. Just as athletes practice in their minds before they step onto the field, you can rehearse your future mentally to build confidence and resilience. Picture yourself staying calm during difficult moments or celebrating small wins along the way. These mental exercises make your vision feel real before it even happens, creating emotional momentum.

Section 2: Aligning Actions with Vision – The Daily Path to Your Future

"Vision without action is merely a dream. Action without vision just passes the time. Vision with action can change the world." —Joel A. Barker

Having a clear vision is a powerful first step, but the magic happens when that vision guides your everyday actions. Dreams stay dreams until they are transformed into consistent habits, decisions, and efforts. Aligning your actions with your vision ensures that every step you take, no matter how small, contributes to the future you want to create.

The Power of Micro-Actions
Big goals can sometimes feel overwhelming. The gap between where you are and where you want to be may seem insurmountable. But success doesn't come from grand gestures—it comes from small, intentional actions repeated consistently.

Micro-actions—like starting the day with five minutes of journaling or choosing to read instead of scrolling social media—may seem insignificant on their own, but they build momentum. These small steps compound over time, slowly but surely moving you closer to your vision.

For instance, consider a writer aiming to finish a book. Rather than focusing on the overwhelming task of completing 80,000 words, they commit to writing just 300 words a day. Over time, these small, consistent efforts accumulate, and before they know it, they've completed their manuscript.

A common mistake people make is waiting for the "perfect moment" to act. But the truth is, there is no perfect moment—there is only now. Aligning with your vision means finding opportunities for progress in the present, no matter how small they appear.

Building a Feedback Loop Between Vision and Action
As you take actions aligned with your vision, you create a feedback loop. Each small success strengthens your belief in the vision, which fuels motivation for the next action. This cycle of action and affirmation helps maintain momentum, even when external validation is lacking.

For example:

- Clarify your vision: Start with a clear image of what you want to achieve.
- Break it down: Identify the habits, skills, or systems needed to support your vision.
- Track progress: Celebrate small milestones along the way to stay encouraged.
- Adjust as needed: Course-correct as you learn from challenges and experiences.

This feedback loop ensures that you stay connected to your vision while building resilience through action. It's okay if the path shifts—what matters is staying committed to the journey.

Embracing Patience with the Process
One of the biggest challenges in aligning actions with vision is patience. We live in a world that rewards instant gratification, but vision-driven action requires playing the long game. The transformation you seek often unfolds slowly, through steady progress. It's essential to trust the process and remain focused, even when results are not immediately visible.

As **James Clear** puts it, **"You do not rise to the level of your goals; you fall to the level of your systems."** Building a life aligned with your vision isn't about bursts of effort—it's about creating systems that support consistency, even on difficult days.

Recalibrating When Life Gets Off Track
No journey is without its detours. Life will throw unexpected challenges your way, and there will be moments when your actions seem out of alignment with your vision. In these moments, it's crucial to show yourself grace. Rather than abandoning the vision, take time to recalibrate.

Ask yourself:

- What small actions can I take today to realign with my vision?
- Are my current routines and habits serving the future I want to create?
- How can I adjust my approach to maintain momentum?

Vision-driven living isn't about perfection—it's about persistence. Even when life gets off track, your vision remains the compass that points you back in the right direction.

Living with Intention Every Day
Aligning actions with vision requires intentionality—choosing to live each day in a way that reflects your values and aspirations. This doesn't mean every moment has to be productive or optimized; it means making deliberate choices that contribute to a meaningful life.

Whether it's taking time for rest, investing in relationships, or pursuing personal growth, every intentional action adds depth and fulfillment to your journey. In the end, success isn't just about reaching a destination—it's about becoming the person capable of building the life you envision.

Section 3: The Power of Reflection – Learning from the Journey

"We do not learn from experience... we learn from reflecting on experience." —John Dewey

In our fast-paced world, it's easy to focus solely on action and progress. But without pausing to reflect, we miss the opportunity to learn from our experiences and grow from our mistakes. Reflection transforms experience into wisdom, helping us stay aligned with our vision and make better decisions moving forward.

Creating Space for Reflection

Reflection doesn't require long hours of introspection; it can be as simple as taking a few moments at the end of each day to ask yourself:

- What went well today?
- What could I have done differently?
- How do today's actions align with my long-term vision?

The key is to create intentional space for reflection. This might mean journaling at night, taking a reflective walk in the morning, or scheduling a weekly check-in to evaluate progress and recalibrate. Reflection helps you become more aware of patterns—both productive and unproductive—and make conscious adjustments.

The Balance Between Action and Reflection
While action moves you forward, reflection ensures you're moving in the right direction. Without reflection, it's easy to get caught in the cycle of doing without purpose. But when balanced with thoughtful reflection, every action becomes more intentional, guiding you toward your desired future.

Consider it like adjusting the sails on a boat—action propels you forward, but reflection ensures you're still heading toward your destination. This balance keeps you aligned with your vision and ensures your efforts remain focused and purposeful.

Learning from Mistakes and Celebrating Wins
Reflection is not just about analyzing mistakes—it's also about celebrating progress. Acknowledging your wins, no matter how small, reinforces positive habits and builds confidence.

At the same time, reflecting on challenges offers valuable lessons. Mistakes aren't failures—they're feedback. When you take time to reflect on what didn't work, you gain insights that help you refine your approach and grow.

Try this simple exercise:

- At the end of each week, write down one thing you're proud of and one thing you could improve.
- Identify a lesson learned from each experience and how you can apply it moving forward.

This habit of learning through reflection ensures that every experience—whether positive or challenging—contributes to your growth.

Reflection as a Tool for Self-Alignment
In life, it's easy to get pulled in many directions, losing sight of what truly matters. Reflection acts as a compass, bringing you back to yourself. It allows you to assess whether your actions align with your values, purpose, and vision.

When you practice reflection regularly, you develop self-awareness. This awareness helps you notice when you're off track and make the necessary adjustments to realign with your path. Reflection isn't about dwelling on the past—it's about learning from it and using those lessons to shape your future.

Section 4: Envisioning Your Future – The Art of Intentional Living

"Go confidently in the direction of your dreams. Live the life you have imagined." —Henry David Thoreau

Your future isn't something you stumble upon—it's something you shape through the choices you make today. Intentional living means crafting a life that reflects your deepest values, goals, and dreams. It's not just about achieving milestones but about showing up each day with purpose, knowing that every action contributes to the person you're becoming.

Aligning Actions with Vision
Living intentionally starts by clarifying your vision. What does your ideal future look like? What kind of person do you want to become? Your daily actions are the brushstrokes that paint that vision into reality. The key is to align each choice with your desired outcome, ensuring that even small steps move you in the right direction.

Here are a few reflective questions to guide your journey:

- Are my current habits aligned with the life I want to create?
- What distractions can I let go of to focus on what truly matters?
- How can I make time for the things that nourish my soul?

When your actions align with your vision, you live with intention, and each day becomes an opportunity to create meaning and fulfillment.

The Power of Micro-Goals and Milestones
Big dreams can feel overwhelming, but breaking them into micro-goals makes the journey more manageable. Each milestone—no matter how small—builds momentum and reinforces progress. Celebrate these moments as reminders that you are moving forward, even when the path feels uncertain.

Think of your life as a garden: each small act—watering a plant, removing a weed, tending to the soil—contributes to a thriving future. The same principle applies to your dreams. Every micro-goal you achieve is a seed planted, nurturing the future you're creating.

Letting Go of the Unnecessary
Part of intentional living is learning to let go. Just as a gardener prunes plants to encourage growth, you must remove anything that no longer serves your journey. This might mean letting go of old habits, beliefs, or relationships that drain your energy.

Letting go isn't about loss—it's about creating space for new opportunities. It's an act of trust, believing that what's meant for you will arrive when you make room for it.

Visualizing Your Ideal Future
Visualization is a powerful tool that bridges imagination with reality. Close your eyes and picture your ideal future in vivid detail—where you are, what you're doing, and how it feels.
Visualization helps your mind and body align with your goals, making them feel tangible and achievable.

Try this practice:

- Each morning, spend five minutes visualizing your ideal day.
- Picture yourself acting with purpose, handling challenges gracefully, and embracing joy in small moments.
- At the end of the day, reflect on how your actions aligned with that vision.

This practice grounds your intentions in your daily reality, helping you move closer to your future with each passing day.

Living Today with Tomorrow in Mind
Intentional living doesn't mean waiting for the future to arrive—it means embodying your vision today. It's about recognizing that the person you aspire to become isn't waiting for you at the finish line—they are forged in each step you take along the way.

Every action, no matter how small, contributes to the legacy you leave behind. When you live with intention, you transform ordinary moments into meaningful ones, building a life that reflects your values and purpose.

Section 5: Leaving a Legacy – Living a Life That Matters

A meaningful life isn't measured by accolades or possessions; it's reflected in the positive impact you have on others. True legacy isn't about what you accumulate but how you inspire, support, and uplift those around you. Living with this awareness shapes your actions today, ensuring that your influence extends far beyond your lifetime.

Think about a teacher who mentors students, not just focusing on grades, but nurturing their passions and growth. Every kind word or piece of advice contributes to the students' journeys long after they leave the classroom, creating a legacy of empowerment and encouragement.

Legacy as Daily Practice
Legacy isn't something you create in a single moment—it's woven through everyday choices. It's the smile you give to a stranger, the patience you show to a friend, the encouragement you offer a colleague. These small moments leave ripples in the lives of others, long after the moment has passed.

Ask yourself:

- What values do I want to leave behind in the hearts of others?
- How can I show up today in a way that reflects those values?

When you live with legacy in mind, your daily actions become opportunities to inspire, motivate, and uplift the people around you.

Empowering Others to Continue Your Work
The most powerful legacy isn't just about what you achieve—it's about the people you empower to carry your vision forward. Great leaders and innovators don't seek to be indispensable; they teach, mentor, and inspire others to rise to their potential.

Think of legacy as a baton in a relay race. Your goal isn't to hold onto it forever—it's to pass it on to the next person, equipped with the skills and confidence to run their part of the journey. The impact you make today lives on in the lives you touch and the lessons you impart.

Alignment Between Purpose and Legacy

Legacy is most meaningful when it reflects your core values. When you align your actions with your purpose, your legacy flows naturally—without the need for elaborate plans or grand gestures. Each moment lived with intention becomes a part of the greater story you leave behind.

This alignment also ensures that your legacy isn't about ego or recognition—it's about authenticity. People will remember the way you made them feel, the guidance you offered, and the example you set through your actions.

The Ripple Effect of a Life Well-Lived
Every action you take today has the potential to spark change in someone else's life. This ripple effect means that even the smallest acts of kindness, courage, or inspiration can carry forward, influencing people you may never meet. Your legacy isn't confined to your immediate circle—it extends into the lives of others through those you inspire.

As **Maya Angelou** wisely said:
"Your legacy is every life you've touched."

When you live with this awareness, each moment becomes an opportunity to create positive change, leaving a lasting impact on the world.

Conclusion: Embracing the Journey of Transformation

As you turn the final pages of this book, it's time to take a moment and reflect on the journey you've just completed—a journey of awakening, self-discovery, and growth. Each chapter has served as a stepping stone, guiding you toward a deeper understanding of yourself and the life you are capable of creating.

You began this journey by waking up to your true potential, breaking free from the unconscious patterns that kept you stuck in a version of yourself that no longer served you. Like Alex and Rachel, who found themselves trapped in comfort and discontent, you've learned that the life you are meant to live isn't defined by external expectations or societal standards. It's shaped by **you**—by your values, your passions, and your unwavering desire to step into the fullness of who you truly are.

The journey of transformation is not linear, nor is it easy. But as you've explored in each chapter, true growth requires leaning into discomfort, confronting limiting beliefs, and continuously realigning your actions with your vision. It's about shedding old layers and embracing the truth that transformation begins from within.

Awakening to Your Inner Drive
In Chapter 1, you explored the importance of understanding your inner drive. The questions that once haunted you—*Is this all there is? Am I truly living the life I was meant to live?*—are no longer points of confusion but starting points for growth. You've discovered that your true power lies not in external achievements but in the clarity of purpose that drives you forward.

By aligning your actions with your deepest values, you've learned to create a life that feels authentic, grounded, and purposeful. You've started to unlock the potential that lies within, no longer chasing after fleeting validation, but building a future rooted in meaning.

Cultivating Resilience and Mastery
From understanding your inner drive, you moved into the realms of mindset and emotional intelligence. In Chapter 2, you embraced the growth mindset—the realization that challenges aren't obstacles but opportunities for growth. This shift has empowered you to see failure not as a reflection of your worth, but as a stepping stone toward mastery.

Mastering self-discipline, as you learned in Chapter 3, isn't about rigid willpower; it's about aligning your habits with the identity of the person you want to become. Small, consistent actions, fueled by a growth mindset, are what build lasting change. And in Chapter 4, you discovered that emotional intelligence—the ability to understand and manage your emotions—wasn't just a skill to be honed but a pathway to deeper, more meaningful relationships.

Living with Purpose and Resilience

In Chapters 5 through 7, you explored the power of living with purpose, positive thinking, and resilience. You learned that purpose provides clarity and direction, aligning your actions with your deeper values. Positive thinking isn't blind optimism, but the ability to reframe setbacks as opportunities for growth. And building resilience has empowered you to thrive through adversity, turning challenges into lessons that fuel your personal transformation.

You now understand that resilience is not about avoiding hardship but about thriving in its face—developing the strength to keep moving forward even when the path isn't clear.

The Art of Decision Making and Creative Power

As you delved deeper, Chapters 8 and 9 invited you to master decision-making and creativity. Decision-making, you learned, is an art—one that requires balancing logic and intuition. By trusting yourself, you've begun making confident choices that align with your values, leaving behind indecision and doubt.

Creativity isn't reserved for artists; it's a fundamental part of your personal evolution. By nurturing your creative instincts and allowing yourself to innovate, you've opened the door to endless possibilities. Each decision you make and each creative endeavor you pursue shapes the life you are building—one that is both imaginative and aligned with your true self.

Leadership, Balance, and Financial Freedom
Chapters 10, 11, and 12 took you on a journey of leadership, work-life balance, and financial well-being. You now understand that leadership isn't about control; it's about influence. It's about empowering others, leading from a place of authenticity, and serving those around you.

Achieving work-life balance isn't about perfect equilibrium; it's about prioritizing what matters most. You've learned to create harmony in your life by making intentional choices, setting boundaries, and dedicating time to what truly brings you fulfillment.

Financial success, as you explored in Chapter 12, isn't just about accumulating wealth—it's about aligning your finances with your values. You now see money as a tool for freedom, growth, and impact, rather than a measure of worth or success. Financial well-being means using resources wisely to build a life that reflects your deepest goals and aspirations.

Continuous Learning and Digital Mindfulness
As you entered Chapters 13 and 14, the focus shifted to lifelong learning and mindful technology use. You've embraced the mindset that learning doesn't stop—it evolves. By cultivating curiosity, you've kept your mind open to new ideas, experiences, and opportunities. You've learned the importance of unlearning old habits and beliefs that no longer serve you, and you now approach each day with the awareness that every moment is an opportunity for growth.

In the digital age, you've learned that technology can either be a tool for distraction or a tool for empowerment. Through mindful engagement with technology, you've taken control of how you interact with the digital world, ensuring it enhances your personal growth rather than detracts from it. You are no longer a passive consumer but an active creator in the digital realm.

Envisioning and Realizing Your Future
Finally, in Chapter 15, you brought it all together by envisioning and realizing your future. You've learned that a powerful vision isn't just a dream—it's a blueprint for intentional living. By reverse-engineering your future, you've broken down your biggest goals into actionable steps, aligning each choice with the future you want to create.

You now see that the life you've been dreaming of is within reach, not because you wish for it, but because you've built it— day by day, decision by decision, moment by moment.

A Life of Purpose, Action, and Legacy
As you move forward from here, remember that this journey doesn't end with the last page. Transformation isn't about reaching a final destination—it's about living with purpose every day, staying committed to growth, and continuously aligning your actions with your vision.

You are now equipped with the tools, mindsets, and habits to create the life you've always wanted—a life that reflects your true potential, your deepest values, and your most authentic self.

But perhaps the most powerful realization you've come to is this: you are already enough. Every step you've taken, every challenge you've faced, has brought you closer to the person you are meant to be. The journey is not about becoming someone new—it's about embracing who you've always been.

As you continue to navigate life's twists and turns, let your vision be your guide, your resilience be your strength, and your purpose be your anchor. And as you grow, remember that your legacy is being woven through every action you take and every life you touch.

This is your hero's journey. The path ahead is yours to walk. Embrace it with courage, knowing that you are fully capable of creating the life you were meant to live.

"Your life is your story, and the adventure ahead of you is the journey to fulfill your own purpose and potential."
— **Kerry Washington**

Have Faith in the Unknown

Be yourself, since everyone else is taken,
Have faith in yourself and the unknown, so you are not forsaken.
In the quiet of your heart, a truth is always waiting,
A light that flickers softly, yet never fading.
There is no map to follow, no path set in stone,
But within, you carry the compass to guide you alone.
The world will offer masks to wear, roles to play,
Yet in your authenticity, you find your own way.
Trust the voice that whispers when the world is loud,
It is the one that knows your worth, beyond the crowd.
For in your essence lies a strength unspoken,
A resilience, a wisdom that cannot be broken.
The unknown may seem vast, its depths uncertain,
But the courage to step forward will draw back the curtain.
Embrace the journey, not the destination,
In each moment, find your own salvation.
No need to fit into another's mold,
For your soul carries stories yet untold.
In the dance of life, be both wild and still,
Let your heart be your guide, and your spirit, your will.
You are enough, as you are, in every way,
So rise with the dawn, and create your own day.

— *Alavida*

Further Reading

For those who wish to explore further into the themes of growth, transformation, and self-discovery, the following books offer valuable insights:

1. **"Atomic Habits" by James Clear**
   A practical and insightful exploration of how small, incremental changes can lead to lasting transformation.

2. **"The Untethered Soul" by Michael A. Singer**
   An invitation to look beyond the noise of the mind and embrace the expansiveness of who we truly are.

3. **"Man's Search for Meaning" by Viktor E. Frankl**
   A profound account of finding purpose and meaning even in the most difficult circumstances, written by a Holocaust survivor and psychologist.

4. **"The Power of Now" by Eckhart Tolle**
   A timeless guide to living in the present moment, free from the chains of past regrets or future anxieties.

5. **"Daring Greatly" by Brené Brown**
   An inspiring look at the power of vulnerability and how it can unlock personal growth and deeper connections with others.

6. **"Deep Work" by Cal Newport**
   A focused guide on how to cultivate deep, meaningful work in a world filled with distractions.

7. **"Grit: The Power of Passion and Perseverance" by Angela Duckworth**

An exploration of how passion and persistence are the keys to long-term success and fulfillment.

8. **"The Four Agreements" by Don Miguel Ruiz**
   A spiritual guide rooted in ancient Toltec wisdom that offers a simple yet profound framework for personal freedom.

9. **"Awaken the Giant Within" by Tony Robbins**
   A motivational classic on how to unlock your personal power and create lasting change in your life.

www.ingramcontent.com/pod-product-compliance
Lightning Source LLC
Chambersburg PA
CBHW070647160426
43194CB00009B/1614